Anxiety in a Relationship

Fear of Abandonment and Insecurity
Often Cause Damage Without Therapy:
Learn How to Identify and Eliminate
Jealousy, Negative Thinking and
Overcome Couple Conflicts

Michelle Martin

Table of Contents

Introduction

"Insecurity kills more dreams than failure ever will." - Suzy Kassem (2011)

Anxiety is a mental illness that you know all too well. You recognize the signs as soon as they begin—lack of concentration, hyperventilating, irritability, sweating, increased heart rate, worry, fear of impending doom, nausea, trembling, and racing thoughts. You dread the moment your anxiety spikes because you struggle to control it, especially when you're in public. You feel that you're the only one dealing with anxiety, but it's the most common form of psychological illness in the United States. These disorders affect over 40 million people 18 years and older every year. Unfortunately, less than 40% seek the help that they need for various reasons, such as lack of health insurance to feeling embarrassed ("Facts & Statistics," n.d.).

You might notice your anxiety creeps up during certain times in your life. For example, when you're about to present to your colleagues, when your professor calls on you to answer a question, or when you're having problems with your significant other. You might also feel anxiety on a daily basis, no matter what you're doing or who you're with. Because anxiety affects millions of people in several areas of their lives, it's important to find a focus for this book. I choose to focus on relationship anxiety because through meeting my with clients, I noticed a pattern emerge from them. I realized that most of the anxiety they felt in their relationship occurred because of past baggage or personal insecurities. As I watched my clients focus on themselves, they started feeling better about their anxiety. They overcame their obstacles by using proven strategies to help decrease anxiety and improve their mindset. Through my book, I strive to give you the same help and results that I've seen throughout my career.

Just like everyone else, you experience insecurities in your relationship, increasing your stress and worries. Some of the most common causes of insecurities include environmental stress, genetics, conflict, worrying about disappointing your partner or someone else, distrust, dependency, and childhood trauma. My book ties together reasons for your insecurity to your anxiety. You can't find strategies to help gain control until you find the root causes.

One of the biggest reasons people carry anxiety into their relationship is fear of abandonment. This fear can stem from feeling abandoned by a parent as a child or for a myriad of other reasons. Some of the biggest signs for this sentiment are feeling separation anxiety, feeling unworthy of love, feeling insecure, sensitivity to criticism, quickly moving on so you don't become attached to one person, and aiming to please.

Jealousy is another common cause that this book will spend a lot of time on. While it's normal to become a little jealous, excessive jealousy can be detrimental to the health of a relationship. For example, studies show that about 90% of men and 60% of women fantasize about someone they've met. However, both 70% of men and women say they've also lied to their partner so they would or wouldn't become jealous (Schwartz, n.d.). But jealousy can quickly become a problem and lead to an unhealthy relationship, which 70% of men and women show because they admitted to lying when it came to a jealous situation in their relationship.

I understand it's not easy to work on problems like jealousy and fear of abandonment, but it's essential to help heal yourself and your relationship. When you're happy, your relationship is happy. This leads to a happy and healthy life and relationship for both you and your partner. But overcoming your issues won't just help your intimate relationship, it'll help relationships with your siblings, parents, friends, coworkers, and anyone else you regularly interact with. As an example of how understanding and overcoming fear can help keep relationships healthy and happy, let's look at an example client of mine with a common story.

A few years ago, Amira, a 20-year-old college student, came to my office. The university counselor sent her my direction because she felt I could better assist her. I could tell she was anxious from the moment I met her because her voice was so soft I could barely hear her when she spoke. She barely shook my hand and I felt her palm was sweaty, all classic signs of anxiety. By the end of our first session, I was amazed by how much I knew about her childhood. She opened up quickly about her father's struggles to hold down a job, his quick temper, and how he had moments where he just "went off." She told me that she never knew when these moments would happen or what would set him off. He could come home and find shoes in the living room instead of the kitchen. Even though her younger brother always left his shows there, that day it became a problem. Sometimes it was a book lying on the end table by the couch. Even if the book was there for days, that day it became a problem. I immediately thought of Post Traumatic Stress Disorder (PTSD) and explained the symptoms to Amira, who informed me her father was a Vietnam War Veteran.

Even though growing up with a father who had undiagnosed PTSD wasn't the only tie to Amira's anxiety, it was a major factor. Once we had a starting point, Amira started putting the pieces together and working toward strategies to help her manage her anxiety. She then started analyzing how her anxiety created an internal fear, especially when it came to men. She talked about how her father's outbursts were stuck in her mind and this caused problems with her spouse. Even though her husband never had outbursts like her father or yelled at her, whenever he was angry, irritable, or just having a bad day she became fearful, anxious, and did her best to stay out of his way.

Because she understood part of the beginning, she began picking up the puzzle pieces and putting them together to create a new whole. She started working through her fear and soon found herself talking out problems with her husband, even when he was irritable or angry.

Once you start reading my book and incorporating it into your life, you'll find yourself picking up the pieces to your puzzle just like Amira. With each piece you put into place, you start to take control and form (what seems like) a new whole. You'll find yourself and your relationships more peaceful and happy. You'll learn more about yourself and develop strategies to ensure you can continue on a brighter journey. You'll also begin to see yourself in a new light. You'll gain confidence, self-esteem, start trusting people, and begin nurturing your new reality. Of course, this doesn't mean that your anxiety is cured, as this isn't truly possible—you learn to control it. Because the anxiety monster is still inside of you, it'll rear its ugly head from time to time, but you'll know how to handle these moments.

My name is Michelle Martin and I am a relationship counsellor from Washington, D.C. As a counselor, I've become acquainted with a wide range of human emotions. Through meeting with my clients and analyzing our sessions, I learned about many behavioral patterns and how they affect relationships. Therefore, I conducted my own study on relationship anxiety, fear of abandonment, pathological jealousy, and unhealthy attachments. The results of this study are presented in my first book—*Anxiety in Relationship*.

The information in this book is a mix of research, real-life scenarios that I faced in my work, and my academic background. My book aims to help you deal with your insecurities and past traumas in much the same way a session with a therapist would.

Chapter 1:

What's Making You Anxious?

As we start our journey together, I want you to remember one fact—you're not alone. Anxiety can make you feel trapped and think that no one understands what you're going through. It's a horrible monster that enjoys dragging you down and placing your mind in solitary confinement. When you find yourself feeling alone, I want you to close your eyes, take a deep breath, and imagine yourself in a peaceful place full of love. Imagine the warmth of the sun as it feels like arms wrapping you up in a hug. Imagine the smell of your favorite flower. You can imagine your family, friends, and anyone else with you smiling as they too feel the warmth and smell the flowers. Hold this image for a few seconds to help you remember you're not alone.

Understanding Anxiety

You know that you have anxiety and it probably affects various parts of your life. For example, you feel anxious at work, driving in bad weather, meeting a new person, or in your relationship. But have you ever truly looked at what anxiety means? Anxiety is your body's natural response to stressful situations, such as public speaking, starting a new job, getting married, or taking a test. This means that, to an extent, it's normal to have anxiety during certain situations.

At this point, you might be asking why anxiety doesn't feel natural. If it's normal to have anxiety during stressful situations, why does it make you feel like something is wrong or you're not doing something right. For instance, you start dating someone who you think is the one. You met them a few weeks ago and talk on the phone daily, but you're getting ready for your next date and feel nauseous. You keep rubbing your palms on the towel because they're sweaty and focus on deep breaths when you feel your heart racing. If anxiety is normal for your body, why are the symptoms hard to handle?

First, it's because you don't truly understand how to control anxiety and what's happening to your body. You don't know where your anxiety stems from or what strategies to use to help you through a stressful situation. Second, your brain isn't wired for you to feel happy, it's wired for your survival. This is why people tend to feel anxiety or like "something bad is going to happen" when they're happy. For example, you survived on negative emotions such as shame and fear throughout your childhood so now your body and mind follows this script. Therefore, when you're happy and feel your life is going well, your mind kicks your anxiety into high gear.

Feeling relationship anxiety is normal, no matter what stage your relationship is in. Not only can it happen when you start dating, but anytime down the road when you're facing a negative event or facing an uncertain future. For example, if you're laid off from your job, you'll start to experience anxiety in your relationship. You and your significant other might start arguing more, especially about finances. You might even question if you're with the right person because you're starting to look at their spending habits in more detail. Plus, stress makes you feel unhappy and this emotion can creep its way into your relationship, causing both you and your partner to feel unhappy in the relationship.

One of the most important factors to remember about relationship anxiety is that it'll pass. These might be words your mother told you when something bad happened and you didn't know how to handle it. It's true and one of the best pieces of advice I can give to my clients—the anxiety and all the emotions with it will pass. The situation that's causing the anxiety will pass. Furthermore, the stress won't cause a profound and long-lasting effect in your relationship. Stress is temporary and one of the best steps you can take is to let it affect you temporarily and then move on.

External Causes of Relationship Anxiety

External causes of anxiety are normal to have in a relationship. They'll last from the time you start dating until the end of your relationship. External causes focus on the forces that aren't in your control, such as work, living arrangement, extended family, or your partner.

It's normal for you to feel more anxiety in your relationship during the beginning because you don't know the person well enough to start letting your guard down yet. This may even be the case when you feel like you're in love with your partner and you begin to wonder if they're the one. You might even dream about marrying them one day and still feel high anxiety. This happens because our hearts tend to work a little faster than our brain. In other words, your brain continues to make you feel anxious while your heart is falling in love. Once your brain catches up with your heart, your anxiety will drop. However, this doesn't mean that you'll never feel anxiety again throughout your relationship. It'll always come and go, depending on several factors.

One of the biggest reasons for anxiety is money, even when bills are paid and you can spend money on items that you don't need. For example, you have enough money to put a downpayment on a new vehicle, trailer, or a boat. Yet, you still feel that you never have enough money or you worry about how you'll pay all your loans if you lose your job. Another way anxiety can rear its ugly head is through differences in spending habits. You might strive to save money while your significant other wants to spend it. You want to support them, but you also want to focus on your financial future. You want security when it comes to retirement and emergencies as they're bound to happen.

Another way finances can cause problems is living situations. For example, you're thinking of moving in together but your partner wants a bigger apartment than what you feel is necessary. You might want to rent an apartment but perhaps your significant other wants to buy a house instead. There are countless ways finances can contribute to anxiety in relationships, so it is imperative you bear these things in mind when making financial decisions in a relationship.

The language your partner uses is another external cause of relationship anxiety. The way your significant other talks and how often can cause anxiety. For example, if you feel that your partner is speaking in a negative or mean tone, you'll struggle to overcome anxiety. If you're an introvert and enjoy spending time alone, having a partner who is talkative and usually by your side can make you feel anxious, especially when you're in the mood to be alone.

Body language is another type of language that can cause anxiety. For example, if your partner talks too widely with their hands or mimics your movements, you can start to feel uncomfortable and this increases your anxiety.

You're on a date with your partner when you notice they're smiling and waving to someone. They come up to your table and your partner introduces them as a coworker. You watch as your partner continues to not only talk to them, but place their hand on their shoulder, joke with them, winks, and shows other signs of frivolous behavior. Your anxiety starts to spike as you wonder how close of friends and coworkers they really are because you don't act toward your coworkers in the same manner. Because of your anxiety, you'll start to pay more attention to how your partner reacts with other people. You'll start to notice every touch and sign of flirting, which will continue to increase your anxiety.

Another big reason for anxiety in the beginning of the relationship is lack of trust. This is usually a temporary issue as once you start to get to know your partner more, you'll start to trust them. When this happens, a lot of the anxiety you feel at the beginning will start to disappear. It's important to note that if you continue to feel anxious because you don't trust your partner, this is a sign of a problem. A few months into your relationship, your trust should be growing stronger. If it's not, you need to reevaluate your relationship.

Stress is a word in life that you can't fully escape. It doesn't matter if you have thousands of dollars in the bank, a great job, and a stable relationship—there will always be stress. Your anxiety will always spike when you feel stressed because it's a normal response to stress. When you're stressed, you're worried about the future or you fear what will happen. You have a feeling of uneasiness that you can't shake and these factors lead you into anxiety territory.

Another common external cause of relationship anxiety is family. In general, any family member can cause a little more stress which leads to anxiety. Some of the family members, such as your children and parents, will have a major influence on your life and therefore cause you to feel more anxious in your relationship from time to time. For example, your children are sick, children aren't doing well in school, or one of your parents needs to go into the nursing home. These are normal factors that bring tension into your relationship, but there are also other family members that can become a central part that isn't normal. For instance, one of your siblings needs a place to stay because they lost a job or one of your close cousins doesn't like your significant other.

Internal Causes of Relationship Anxiety

Even if you've found the love of your life, you'll still have anxiety. Unfortunately, there is no cure for relationship anxiety because there are always external causes that you can't control. However, you should always be aware of the second type of anxiety—internal causes, which you can control. Unlike external causes, the anxiety you feel from internal causes will cause so much strain on your relationship that you'll find it crumbling around you. You could find someone you could never imagine living without, but your anxiety doesn't allow you to have a strong hold on the relationship. Just like external causes, there are several internal causes.

Past trauma and abuse is one of the biggest reasons for internal causes. For example, you recently left an abusive relationship and find yourself worrying that your new partner will start abusing you in the same way. You fear what'll happen during your first disagreement. Your past abuse might stem from your childhood, so when your partner becomes angry it reminds you of being slammed against the wall or pushed down and you fear your partner will perform the same action. Even if you've been dating for years, you can still find yourself struggling with the past abuse and trauma.

Just like past trauma can cause anxiety in your relationship, so can past relationship failures. You've probably had a relationship in the past that you thought was going to last for the rest of your life, but soon found yourself alone. You and your partner might have gone separate ways physically or emotionally. Either way, it's hard to find yourself alone and learning to trust yourself or get out in the dating scene again isn't easy, especially if it's been a while. You might find yourself questioning what you can do differently now so you can ensure that this relationship lasts.

It's important to note that past trauma or relationship failures can cause another internal issue—fear of abandonment or worrying that your partner will leave you. No one wants to feel like they'll live alone the rest of their life, so when you've felt this before you worry about it happening again. Fear of abandonment can strike if you felt alone most of your life, especially in your childhood. It can also happen if one or both of your parents left you and never returned. But, a fear of abandonment can happen without any past trauma or relationship failures. Psychologically, you need human interaction. You need to become attached to someone because your brain is wired this way. Therefore, when you feel that someone might leave, you become worried and your anxiety spikes.

Fear also increases your anxiety by worrying that you'll get hurt or lose something that feels good. You want to feel that you're not only wanted but needed by your partner. You want to feel the love and passion that they have for you. Yet, you're anxious about these feelings because you can lose them and this will result in you getting hurt.

Another way that fear interrupts your peaceful nature and causes anxiety is through rejection. You don't want to feel that someone doesn't want to spend time with you or doesn't like you enough. Even if you're not sure that you want to become intimate with the person yet, you still have a fear of rejection and this causes you to protect yourself in many ways. You might find yourself backing away from a relationship that's getting serious because of the anxiety you feel. You might also find yourself doing everything for your partner and pushing your needs and wants aside. You believe if you focus all of your attention on what your partner needs and wants, they won't reject you.

The attention you place on your partner can turn into another internal struggle known as jealousy. While a little jealousy in your relationship is normal and healthy, it can easily spiral out of control. When you mix jealousy with lack of trust and self-esteem, it becomes one of the biggest struggles in relationship anxiety. Think of it this way—when you're jealous, you fear the worst. For example, your partner says they're going out to the bar with their friend but you imagine them meeting another person and cheating on you. When they come home late, you start questioning them and accuse them of cheating. Soon, your argument is out of control and you're losing sight of the love that your partner still has for you. Jealousy can also cloud the love that you have for your partner.

Finally, another big internal cause of relationship anxiety and one reason that often attaches itself to other causes is low self-esteem. When you have low self-esteem, it's hard for you to believe that anyone will treat you well. You expect the worst from people and you believe that you deserve the worst. You might even find yourself questioning how someone could truly love you. You might start to believe that your partner is using you for their personal needs and will "toss you to the side" when they have what they want. There are a lot of negative thoughts that associate themselves with low self-esteem and this creates anxiety.

What Questions Should You Be Asking Yourself?

Now, before you move on to addressing relationship anxiety, it's time to reflect and ask yourself a series of questions. The questions you ask yourself will depend on your experiences and causes of relationship anxiety (or what you believe to be your causes). You can start with a series of general questions that everyone should ask themselves and then move on to the personal questions. When you come to this point, reflection is necessary. You've learned a variety of causes, but not all of them will resonate with you. You need to focus on the causes that you feel are a part of your puzzle. Ask yourself why you feel a certain cause is a part of your life and look at ways that you feel you can start to overcome them.

But first take a step back from your reflection and start with some of these general questions as they'll help lead you into your personal questions.

You need to ask yourself, "Do I see something developing from my relationship in the long run?" This is an important question to ask at the beginning of the relationship before you devote too much time to making it work. Like most people, you're more likely to become attached to the person when you put energy and time into the relationship. The more energy you give your partner, the harder it is to leave them. Reflect on your relationship now and think about your future. Do you see your partner supporting you in your dreams? Do they want to see you succeed? Do you see yourself marrying your partner and growing old with them?

Next, you should ask yourself, "Is my relationship worth working on?" It's important to ask yourself this question more than once as most people feel like they have the best relationship in the world at the beginning—meaning your answer is yes. But once you're a couple of months into the relationship, you might give yourself a different answer. When you consider if it's worth working on your relationship, you need to look at several factors. First, you need to think about your goals and how they fit into your partner's vision and the relationship in general. For instance, if you notice your partner doesn't support your goals, it's time to look at how your relationship will affect your path in life and if this is something you want to change. You also need to decide if the change is worth it.

A third question to ask is "Do I feel anxious because of my partner's actions or my own fears or baggage?" Sometimes it's hard to determine what the underlying cause of anxiety is and you need to take some time to reflect. You might even find yourself talking to a family member, friend, or a professional who can help you sort through your anxiety. However, you can usually gain an idea of what is making you anxious by thinking about the situation that happened before you started to feel your anxiety. For example, you're having a discussion with your partner when it starts to become heated and you feel it turning into an argument. Immediately, you start to feel your anxiety rise so you back away from your partner and tell them that you need some space. You fear where the argument can go so you feel it's best for you to have some time alone. While you're alone, you start to reflect on how a friendly discussion turned into a heated argument and why you became anxious. You think about your partner's past actions during an argument and realize there's no reason to feel fear. Your mind then takes you back to your childhood when you saw your parents arguing. You remember your father yelling at your mom, who just sat quietly at the table. You even remember a couple of times where your father slammed his fist on the table, which made your mother jump. By reflecting on your anxiety, you learn that it stems from your past and emotional baggage you carry from your childhood.

After your reflection, you'll find your weaknesses that lead to your anxiety. Once you do, it's time to ask yourself, "Am I willing to address my weaknesses and work through my fears for my relationship?" You need to admit to your weaknesses and learn to overcome them because ignoring them won't help you or your relationship. In a sense, you need to ask yourself if you're willing to work on yourself for your partner. It's not easy to focus on your weaknesses and you'll find yourself struggling for several reasons. You might even find yourself sad or sinking into a depression as you start working on strengthening your weaknesses. However, once you make it to the other side, you'll feel like a new person. This doesn't mean you won't have weaknesses as they are a part of life. But, by working on them, you're working on a better life for yourself, your partner, and your future family.

Another question to ask yourself is "Who do I want to become?" It's important to have your ideal or highest self in mind so you can start working towards who you want to be. In any relationship, you need to be happy with yourself. If you're not happy then your relationship will struggle. Sometimes, becoming happy means you need to change your mindset, such as turning your negative thoughts into positive ones. Other times it means that you need to change your career path or make another life changing decision. Even if you don't feel that your relationship is worth the change, let go of focusing on your relationship and focus on you.

The questions above will give you an idea about your current state of affairs. They'll let you dissect what you're going through so you can realize if it's something temporary or if your relationship is worth keeping. It's important not to just look at your partner when you're analyzing your relationship but you can't just look at yourself either. Always remember, there are two people when it comes to making a relationship work and you both need to put forth the effort or your relationship will become lost in the shuffle.

Chapter 2:

Anxious Attachment: What Is It and Has It Ruined Your Chances of Love?

Once you have the basis of your anxiety, (i.e., the underlying causes and how they affect your relationship) it's time to start digging a bit deeper into the psychological concepts and how they determine your attachment style.

Theory of Attachment

Psychiatrist John Bowlby was the first person to look at attachment theory through his seminal work during the mid-1900s. Bowlby worked at a Child Guidance Clinic in London. He worked closely with emotionally disturbed children and this brought him to focus on a child's attachment to their parents. From here, Bowlby noted that many children who had already formed attachment issues had parents who suffered from their own attachment problems.

Some of Bowlby's most influential studies on attachment occurred during the 1950s. He worked alongside psychologist James Robertson to study how distressed children became when they were separated from their mothers. They focused on all aspects of the children's wellbeing from their cognitive to emotional development. After a 1952 study, the researchers concluded that children felt psychological and emotional distress when separated from their mothers, even when another caregiver fed them or tried to decrease their anxiety through play or other means (McLeod, 2017).

Mary Ainsworth is another pioneer psychologist. As a colleague to Bowlby, Ainsworth started looking at the infant and parent separations. Along with her students, Ainsworth developed a laboratory paradigm called "strange situation" which looks at the relationship between an infant up to the age of 12 months and their parent. During the study, the participants were brought to the lab and placed under surveillance. The researchers would separate the infants from their parents for a period of time and then reunite them. Ainsworth repeated this process several times so her students could observe and record how the infants handled their parents leaving and what happened on their return (Fraley, 2018).

The study concluded by supporting Bowlby's theory with close to 60% of the infants becoming upset when their parent left and then happy when the parent returned. They felt comfort from their parents and showed a pattern of secure behavior. Less than 20% of the infants became upset when their parents left and then showed signs of distress. Once their parents returned, they struggled to comfort their babies. In response, the infants showed that while they wanted to be soothed by their parents, they also wanted to push them away because their parents left them. Ainsworth classified these infants as 'anxious-resistant.' A third type, classified as 'avoidant,' held about 20% of the infants. These babies didn't seem too bothered when their parents left the room. They would engage in play with other people or toys. Even when their parents returned, the infants didn't seem to need their comfort as they usually continued to play (Fraley, 2018).

In the 1980s, psychologists Cindy Hazan and Phillip Shaver took these studies a bit further. They became the first psychologists to look at attachment styles in adulthood. They looked at how the emotional bond adults held in their romantic relationships related to their childhood. In conclusion, Hazan and Shaver noticed several similarities between adult romantic partners and the infant-parent relationship. First, both relationships engage in close contact with each other. Second, both relationships have their own "baby talk" language. Third, they both discover characteristics about the other person. Fourth, both parties feel safe when the other person is close to them. Fifth, both parties show signs of insecurity when the other person is not in close contact with them. Finally, both engage with facial features, notice body language, and generally interact with each other in various ways (Fraley, 2018).

Since the publication of these landmark studies, psychologists continue to look into attachment between humans and how certain situations can affect people throughout their lives. Today, psychologists confirm that attachment theory is a type of generational trauma. This means that problems with attachment tend to follow families from generation to generation until one person tries to stop the cycle, similar to stopping the cycle of abuse. For example, if your mother felt neglected by her mother as a child, you're more likely to feel neglected by your mother because she'll follow a similar trend. This trend can continue until someone changes its direction and finds a way to end the neglect and the attachment style that follows.

The theory of attachment is important in the psychological field because, as Ainsworth and her students proved, there are different types of children and they react differently when their parents leave. This shows that there are not only different attachment styles, but different causes of those attachment styles as well. Furthermore, the study laid the groundwork for future psychologists to look deeper into how the parent-child relationship affects attachment styles, how it can change a child's style, and how this style can affect them throughout their life.

It's important to note that attachment theory is still in its infancy. Researchers continue to conduct studies focusing on the topic and there are still many questions that don't have answers. While this doesn't change the styles of attachment, it does mean that additional information can be added in the future as studies will continue to search for answers to questions.

Different Attachment Styles

Before you discover your attachment style, it's important to have an understanding of the different attachment styles. There are four main styles and they each affect your relationship a bit differently. It's important to note that each style has positive and negative features. This means it's up to you to ensure that you focus on creating a healthy attachment instead of focusing on the negative or unhealthy characteristics.

I also want to stress that no matter where you find yourself, it's always important to work on creating the best relationship possible with your partner. Even if you find yourself in the secure attachment style, which is considered the healthiest style, you need to focus on making sure that you and your partner work together so you can continue having a strong relationship. But you also need to remember that you're not in charge of your partner's actions. You can't control what your significant other does—you can only control what you do. If you find yourself in an unhealthy attachment style, don't become discouraged. Take a step back and reflect on the reasons why you're sitting here and look for ways to improve your style. For example, you might start understanding yourself better by reading this book or you might seek a professional therapist to help you work through past trauma. Whatever step you take down the road, be proud of yourself for taking it. Reaching out for help is one of the biggest personality strengths a person can possess.

The *secure attachment style* is seen as one of the healthiest styles. You have a high level of emotional intelligence, which means you're aware of your emotions and how to handle them. You don't often let your emotions "run wild" or control you because you know how to take a step back and focus on remaining calm when angry or showing a smile when you're feeling down. However, this can also mean that you tend to hide your true emotions from your partner, which can have negative effects on your relationship. The more open and honest you are about what you're feeling, the stronger relationship you'll have.

You don't tend to avoid your emotions in your relationship. When something is bothering you, it's easy to talk to your significant other because you feel comfortable and you don't fear rejection. You also don't worry about your partner abandoning you.

While you feel anxiety in your relationship, it isn't often or severe. You're not an anxious person and you tend to go with the flow. You usually have a feeling that everything will work out for the best. When you do start to feel anxiety, you usually control it and open up to your partner about your emotions. This strength in communication will help keep your relationship strong and healthy.

You're dependent on your partner and you let them be dependent on you. You know when your significant other needs you and you'll do your best to ensure you're there for them. You're also attuned to your partner's emotions and usually know when something is wrong because you just "feel it." Because you understand that it can take time for your significant other to open up, you don't push them. Instead, you let them know you're there for them when they're ready to talk to you. You're patient, understanding, and forgiving.

When it comes to your children, you have a very warm and compassionate relationship with them. You make them feel secure. You understand what your child needs and you'll do anything you can to ensure they get what they need.

Dismissive-avoidant attachment style means that you're emotionally distant with your partner. You tend to keep them at a certain length so you can protect yourself and your emotions better. You're known to reject close intimacy, which causes your partner to want to become closer to you.

'Independence' is a strong word in your vocabulary. In fact, one reason you refuse to become too close to your significant other is because you feel that intimacy takes away some of your independence. You also don't let yourself become dependent on your partner.

You communicate with your partner, but you avoid talking about your emotions. You're seen as a stoic person because you're in control of your emotions, but it's mainly because you avoid them. You don't like to focus on what you're feeling. You also don't like discussing your partner's emotions and will find a way to change the subject if they bring them up.

Due to your lack of showing emotion, you're good at remaining in control during stressful situations. Even when your anxiety spikes, you can keep your emotions in check and this helps you develop a plan of action. You're known to take charge when there's a crisis.

You crave alone time and would rather sit in a room by yourself focusing on your projects than watching a movie with your partner. This alone time not only affects your intimate relationship, but also the relationship with your children. Because you're emotionally distant with yourself, you can't be emotionally there for them. This causes your children to become detached from their emotions, carrying on the dismissive-avoidant attachment style.

Fearful-avoidant attachment style is sometimes referred to as unresolved or disorganized attachment style. This is when you let fear control your relationship and you struggle to become close to anyone because of past traumas and abuse. You haven't worked through your past traumas or mourned any loss, so you're still attached to the past and this leads to a lot of problems in your current relationships.

You can't handle when people become close to you. In fact, if you feel they're coming too close you'll start to become irritated. You'll become argumentative and even show rage because you're unable to control your emotions. You're afraid that any new relationship will follow the same pattern as your past ones, which were dysfunctional and unhealthy.

You may struggle with mental illness, such as Post Traumatic Stress Disorder (PTSD), Anxiety Disorder, or Depression. You tend to disassociate from your emotional pain and will avoid anything that sets off your triggers. For example, in order to avoid the emotional pain you have left over from an abusive relationship, you'll avoid starting another intimate relationship.

Some people see you as narcissistic because you tend to only worry about yourself, but sometimes this is more of your defense mechanism from the world. However, you can easily develop Narcissistic Personality Disorder without psychological treatment to help you overcome your past traumas. You're antisocial and lack empathy.

The same treatment you received as a child, you'll bring on your own children. You're unable to care for them from an emotional standpoint and often react in anger. Your children will struggle developing a connection to you, which will follow them in their future relationships.

Anxious-preoccupied attachment style means that you have a lot of anxiety. You struggle with intimate relationships because you're afraid of being rejected and you're needy. This can make your partner feel that you're too clingy or dependent. You also become preoccupied with the relationship, which can lead to an obsession in making sure everything is going well. Unfortunately, the more you focus on your relationship, the worse your anxiety becomes.

You're quick to blame yourself for everything that goes wrong and you expect the worst. However, you can also turn around and blame other people for your mistakes because you become worried about the outcome of your mistake. This makes it hard for you to trust other people because you feel you can't trust yourself. If you're with someone who can't control their anger or is highly sensitive, you tend to take what they say and do personally, which causes you to become more seclusive.

You're highly emotional and struggle to control your emotions, which can cause various problems in your relationship. You don't set good boundaries and are seen as highly moody. Many people tend to look at you at someone who likes to "stir the pot" and create drama. While this is usually unintentional, you do tend to connect with conflict.

When it comes to your relationship with your children, you're unable to give them the peaceful structure that they need. They'll struggle to make decisions because they become anxious about making a mistake. They worry about your anger or moodiness, so they'll keep their distance from you.

What Is Your Attachment Style?

Now that you have a run-down of the four main attachment styles, it's time to focus on your style. You might have an idea after reading a description of the four, but the best way to make sure is to complete a quick psychological quiz that'll help you determine your relationship attachment style.

There are a number of quizzes that you can complete online on sites like testyourslf.psychotest.com or Science of People. However, I'll give you an example test so you can get an idea about your attachment style without having to go anywhere else. It's important to note that all the quizzes follow a general guideline which leads to your attachment style. This means that the answers you give will determine your style. Therefore, it's important that you're as honest as possible when answering the questions. Once you get your answer, you can start learning more about why you're a certain style and what you can do to overcome your challenges and create a stronger relationship.

Attachment Style Quiz

For each statement, circle the answer that best fits you.

1. I depend on people easily.
   - Disagree
   - Agree
2. I feel nervous/anxious when my partner gets too close to me.
   - Disagree
   - Agree
3. I develop emotional connections easily with other people.
   - Disagree
   - Agree
4. I worry that my partner will stop loving me.
   - Disagree
   - Agree
5. If my partner starts pushing me for commitment, I start to become anxious.
   - Disagree
   - Agree
6. I start to question my relationship when my partner and I argue.
   - Disagree

- Agree

7. I struggle to support my partner when they're emotionally down.
    - Disagree
    - Agree

8. I always try to fix someone else's problem.
    - Disagree
    - Agree

9. I worry that I care more for my partner than they care for me.
    - Disagree
    - Agree

10. I don't feel comfortable talking about how I feel with my partner.
    - Disagree
    - Agree

11. I struggle with letting my walls down.
    - Disagree
    - Agree

12. I feel the urge to end my relationship when it becomes too intimate.
    - Disagree
    - Agree

13. I worry that my partner won't care for me once they get to know the real me.
    - Disagree
    - Agree

14. My independence is more important than my relationships.
    - Disagree
    - Agree

15. If my partner starts to act distant, I worry that I did something wrong.
    - Disagree
    - Agree

16. I worry that if my partner isn't near me, they'll find someone else.
    - Disagree
    - Agree
17. I get over a relationship quickly after a breakup.
    - Disagree
    - Agree

To score your test, you need to measure the number of agrees and disagrees you have. For instance, if more than six of your answers are "agree" you have an anxious attachment style. Around 15 to 20% of the population falls into this category (Edwards, n.d.). In general, it means that you're insecure in your relationships and you tend to overly worry. When you're looking for a partner, you'll try to find someone who will 'complete' you or someone who has a complementary personality. For example, you'll find someone who doesn't show a lot of anxiety and remains in control. You also have a feeling that you need someone who is intimate with you, even if you're not comfortable with intimacy. In other words, you feel better when you have a significant other than when you're alone.

If you answered "disagree" to most of the questions, your attachment style is secure and you don't have a lot of anxiety when it comes to your relationships. Most of the population maintains a secure attachment style. Even if your attachment style is secure, you still want to focus on techniques to help control anxiety in your relationship. Anxiety is an issue that likes to jump into people's minds and create chaos when everything is going well. Even if you've been in a relationship for years and have noticed very little anxiety, it can still increase over time because of certain life events. For instance, growing old creates a strong fear in people because they start to worry more about their loved one and what they'll do if something happens to them. Therefore, even if you fall under the secure attachment style, don't stop reading this book because there are a lot of techniques that can help you continue to control anxiety or know what to do when it does pop into your relationship.

So, You're Under the Anxious Attachment Category

When most people find themselves in the anxious attachment category, they start to become worried. They worry about how their partner views them and wonder if they'll ever be able to change. In fact, you're probably feeling a little anxious right now and wondering what you can do to aim yourself toward the secure attachment style. First, I want you to realize that it is possible to go from anxious to secure, but it takes a lot of time and a lot of work. You also need to understand why and how your attachment style affects you before you can start looking at changing your direction.

Before I take you on a tour of the effects of anxious attachment style in a relationship, I want you to understand two important points. First, you need to realize that you're desperate to find your 'fairytale' love story. This means that you'll continue to find something wrong with your partner or you'll feel that they're not good enough for you until you find your fairytale. Unfortunately, the fairytale love story you're looking for doesn't exist. There is no perfect person, there's only a perfect person for you. This means that your perfect partner will still have faults. They'll still drive you nuts, cause anxiety, and sometimes it'll feel like they don't listen to you. There will be days where you become so frustrated because you feel unheard or that they don't understand your emotions. No matter how strong they are at communicating, this is all part of regular frustrations in a relationship. In a sense, you need to expect it so you can find your perfect partner.

Second, you need to remember that you're naturally going to look for someone who completes you. This isn't just because you fell under the anxious category as even secure people will try to find someone who completes them. The trick is to change your mindset when it comes to the word 'complete.' Now, you're looking for someone to have a relationship with because you don't like to be single. You feel that you need someone, so you'll find anyone who will fill this void. To work on becoming more secure, you need to become comfortable with being alone. This might mean you stay single and live alone for awhile. Once you realize that you're perfectly capable of being single, you can start looking at what the word 'complete' means to you and your relationship. For example, maybe you want someone who is handy around the home because you don't know how to fix a sink, toilet, or other home appliance. You might also feel that 'complete' means someone who works hard and is dedicated in their career path.

Effects of Anxious Attachment on a Relationship

You know that you have an anxious attachment style when it comes to your relationships. You also have an idea of what this means, but you might still wonder what the effects of this type of style will have on your mental and emotional health along with your relationship.

One of the key factors to remember as you read about the effects is that you can change your attachment style. You can work through your past trauma and start to heal. From there, you can walk down a path toward secure attachment. The trick is you need to make the choice. You need to decide if you want to stay where you are and face the effects below or if you want to work toward healing.

One of the biggest effects is anxiety. You're going to feel nervous about nearly everything that happens in your relationship and even situations that might not happen. For example, you have an overwhelming fear that you won't get pregnant. You and your partner have tried to have a baby for a few months but nothing has happened. You're afraid to go to the doctor because you don't want to hear that you're infertile. This might cause your partner to leave you and then you'll truly be alone for the rest of your life. Even if this scenario seems a bit excessive to you now, the longer you allow your anxiety to control your life, the worse it becomes.

If you're looking for a new relationship, you notice that your nerves keep you up at night. Every time you feel that you're falling in love with someone, you start to become so anxious that you need to break it off. It's not that you really fear the relationship, it's more that you expect the worst. You fear that it won't work so why should you even try. The longer you allow this thinking to be a part of your life, the less positively you'll think. Eventually, your mind will only think negatively.

Another massive issue is fear of abandonment. This can tie into your fear of having a relationship by making you feel it's better to not start a relationship because they'll leave you anyway. However, once you begin a relationship your fear will turn into how you'll live without them. You can become so afraid of them abandoning you that you unknowingly keep them too close to you. You make it nearly impossible for them to think they can leave you and this forms an unhealthy and abusive relationship for both of you.

When your anxiety starts to control your life, you'll find yourself always on edge. Every problem, even the smallest ones, will seem like the worst problem in the world. Of course, this only increases your fears and makes your emotions uncontrollable. When a discussion arises you'll no longer find yourself capable of talking rationally or calmly. You'll be unable to find a way to compromise with your partner. Instead, you'll find yourself having emotional outbursts that can become physical.

As you continue to let your anxiety take control, you'll find yourself needing constant affection. You'll wonder why your partner didn't text you "good morning" or kiss you before they left for work. You'll contact them and question them about it, expecting them to say the worst. You'll start to worry when they don't communicate with you right away or wonder why they don't call you back when they're supposed to. Your mind won't take you to a rational explanation that they're busy at work and will contact you as soon as they can. Your mind will make you imagine the worst possible scenario.

You'll have a desire to control everything about your relationship. You'll start to feel that by controlling the relationship, you can ensure that your partner won't leave you. You believe you can protect yourself from getting hurt in any way. Unfortunately, by doing this, you're not noticing the emotional and psychological pain you're causing your significant other.

Your intimate relationship also won't be the only relationship that suffers. If you have children, your relationship with them will struggle as well. Even your immediate family and friends will start to notice a change and find themselves doing what they can to keep their distance from you.

Your jealousy will spike and you could turn into someone that you never imagined. You might find yourself believing your partner is cheating on you. You might accuse them even though you have no proof. It can come to the point where you don't even hear them when they tell you that they're not cheating on you because you've made yourself believe it. Avoiding this spiral of jealous behavior is critical to addressing unhealthy forms of attachment and redirecting your relationship to a healthier place

Chapter 3:

Jealousy: Why It Happens and

What You Can Do About It

Experiencing jealousy in your relationship is normal. While it shouldn't happen often, it's normal to get a little jealous when your partner is talking to someone else more or they're discussing how gorgeous they think someone is. When it comes to this type of jealousy, it's nothing to worry about. Even if you don't want to feel jealous, it's normal and can even be healthy for your relationship. However, jealousy can quickly ruin your relationship and even the lives of others (including you) when it becomes a major problem. When you start acting on your jealousy in a negative way, it starts to become a problem. When you feel the need to control all of your partner's actions so you can make sure that they're not doing something they shouldn't, your relationship is becoming unhealthy.

Just like you did earlier, you need to focus on asking yourself questions related to your jealousy. First, you should ask yourself, "Is my jealousy over something that my partner has said or done?" If your answer is yes, dig a little deeper to what they said or did. Ask yourself if it's worth talking to your partner about or if you're just overreacting. Don't try to push your jealousy off as 'silly' if you're really bothered by what happened. The only way you'll be able to move forward and stop yourself from becoming jealous the next time is by communicating with your partner.

The next question you need to ask yourself is, "Am I jealous because of past trauma, abuse, or low self-esteem?" No matter what you answered to the first main question, you need to answer this question as well. The reality is, you can feel jealous over something your partner said because of an event from your past. The only way you'll truly know why you feel a certain way is by understanding where your emotions and thoughts come from. The only way you can find this out is by asking yourself questions, even if the answers become painful.

Signs of an Unhealthy Relationship Because of Jealousy

Before you learn about the causes of jealousy and how to overcome them, it's important to understand the signs of an unhealthy relationship because of jealousy. When you hear that pangs of jealousy are normal for a relationship, it's hard to distinguish when it's healthy and when it's unhealthy. Through psychological studies and observations with my clients, I've come up with a list of signs to help you know when your relationship has hit the unhealthy path and it's time to make some changes.

One sign that jealousy is making your relationship unhealthy is you feel your partner needs to spend all of their time with you. You understand that this isn't reasonable, but it's what you feel. For example, you might question them about where they went if they didn't come home from work at their regular time. You might need to know everything they're doing during the evenings and weekends, especially if they're not working or have a prior commitment. This level of jealousy can get to the point where you start asking your partner to cancel certain commitments so you can spend time with them.

Another sign is that you're trying to get your partner to listen to rules about who they can and can't talk to. For example, you become jealous when you see them talking to their co-worker because you feel they're flirting and tell your partner that you don't want them talking to their co-worker unless it's about work. It doesn't matter who the person is, if you become jealous you'll ask your partner to stop talking to them. Mentally, you might realize that your requests are unreasonable, but your emotion of jealousy is stronger than you can handle so you find yourself making the rule.

You feel suspicious about everything your partner does when you're not around. Because jealousy is a large part of your anxiety, you find yourself imaging the worst. For example, you might worry your partner is having an affair at work. You imagine that they meet for lunch in a private location so no one suspects what's happening. You worry about why they want to do something without you, even if it's run to the post office or the store. Even when you find yourself trying to trust your partner or telling yourself that there's no reason you should be suspicious, your emotions are out of your control so you continue to make rules and become possessive.

When you're in a healthy relationship, you protect your partner. When you're in an unhealthy relationship, you're possessive of your partner. For example, you give your partner something of yours that they have to wear at all times. Even if you're married, you don't feel that their wedding ring is enough, so you give them a necklace, bracelet, or something else. When you're out in public you show a lot of affection. You want the world to know that your partner is yours and they're not allowed to go near them.

You'll start manipulating your partner so they feel a certain way and do what you ask, even if it's irrational. For example, you might make them feel that they need to stop bowling with their friends on Sunday nights because your ex would come home drunk and abuse you. You tell them that every Sunday you fear this will repeat. You explain that you're trying to work through this issue because you know they're not your ex, but you need time. You might also tell them that if they truly love and care for you, they'll stop going bowling and help you work through your past trauma.

You walk into your bedroom and notice your partner has left their phone on the bed. You quickly grab it and read their messages, check their internet history, and note who they've called and how long they talked. You feel that you need to see this information as it'll help you learn whether they're cheating on you, following the rules, or what they're truly up to.

Jealousy is one of the most powerful emotions that can quickly destroy a relationship. It's hard for many people to understand the line between normal jealousy and when you're going too far. By noting some of the most common signs of an unhealthy relationship, you can start to understand where your relationship stands and start focusing on ways to manage your jealousy.

Jealousy vs. Fear of Abandonment

Before you read about the primary causes of jealousy, I want to bring one important note to your attention—jealousy and fear of abandonment are not the same. There are a lot of people who connect the two, but you can have one without the other. Of course, you can also find yourself struggling with both characteristics, but this doesn't mean that they stem from the same past issue.

To help you distinguish jealousy from fear of abandonment (which I will discuss in the following chapter), remember that jealousy is the result of latent paranoia. When you're jealous you struggle with trusting and truly connecting to someone. On the other hand, fear of abandonment starts because you worry that your partner is becoming distant. You start to believe that you feel the end of the relationship looming above your head and you want to do everything you can to avoid it. Fear of abandonment is a stronger feeling and brings you to a psychologically deeper level than jealousy.

Many people find it easy to confuse jealousy and fear of abandonment because you're afraid of your partner leaving you, usually for someone else. If you're like most people, you take the fear you feel as jealousy instead of what it is—fear of abandonment. You worry that your partner will leave you for someone else, even an ex that they don't talk to anymore. It's easier to say that you're jealous instead of saying that you fear them abandoning them for various reasons. First, you understand jealousy easier than fear of abandonment. Second, you don't like admitting that you're vulnerable enough to fear that your significant other will leave you. Don't be ashamed about the second reason because it's just as normal as the first. It's all part of your anxiety in your relationship.

To understand why you combine the two, you'll need to take a journey into your past. You'll need to ask yourself questions and look at why you mistake jealousy for fear of abandonment. You might quickly realize the reason is because many people have abandoned you throughout your life. You might find yourself struggling to understand your reason because it's hard to look into your past or you can't place your finger on it. One of the most important steps you can take in this process is not pushing yourself. You don't need to find an answer right away. In fact, it'll probably take you a few days or even a couple of months. Sometimes getting to know yourself and understanding where your anxieties stem from takes a lot of patience and reflection.

Another way you'll learn to understand the difference is by understanding each feature and its causes. By learning about jealousy and what the main causes are, you can start to connect them to your life. For example, you might realize that you have personal insecurities and this leads to low self-esteem. These are a couple of primary causes of jealousy and don't have much to do with fear of abandonment.

Primary Causes of Jealousy in a Relationship

There are many causes of jealousy in a relationship. You might have some of these causes on the list and you might not. You might realize that the main cause for your jealousy is personal to you and deals with an event that occurred in your childhood that's not on this list. Because everyone's story is different, I can't fit every single primary cause of jealousy in a relationship in this list. However, I can discuss some of the most common reasons and then help you make connections and learn what you can do to manage your jealousy. I say manage because jealousy isn't something that you can cure. It's not like the flu or cold where you can take medication or build up your immune system to get rid of it. Like learning disabilities and other mental health issues, you take time to educate yourself on the topic and use techniques so you can manage your reactions. In a sense, you learn how to live with your jealousy by controlling it instead of letting it control you.

One of the biggest reasons you feel jealous is due to lack of self-confidence. Even though you attribute your jealousy to your partner's behavior, it's only part of the reason. Think of the behavior from your significant other as the trigger that releases your lack of self-confidence. Even if you usually feel good about yourself and others view you as having a healthy level of self-confidence, you can doubt your skills and abilities in your relationship. You might feel that you and your partner don't have a strong connection like you used to. You might notice that they're talking to other people more or going out with friends. They might be working longer hours or your relationship has hit a bump in the road. Each one of these situations can damage your self-confidence in your relationship. It's natural for one person to start to question if they're doing everything they can to keep their partner happy, so when you start to feel that they're not as happy as they used to be, you blame yourself.

Your lack of self-confidence can come from fear. This is different from fear of abandonment because you're not directly worried about them leaving you. Your fear can arise because you're worried your relationship is in a rocky place or that you're not doing everything you can. Of course, the fear can lead to fear of abandonment as you can become afraid of being left alone.

Another reason is because of personal insecurities. You might worry about your partner cheating on you because your ex cheated. You might worry about your significant other abusing you because this has happened in the past. Your personal insecurities can come from any point in your life and you might not even realize they're the reason for your jealousy. The trick is understanding your insecurities so you can start to overcome them. Like most people, you've learned to live with them so you don't always realize they're a part of you.

Projection is another cause of jealousy. Projection is a psychological term that means you perceive your emotions in someone else, such as your partner. It's considered a defense mechanism and something that you do without knowledge because you don't want to face the emotions yourself. For example, when your partner talks to people at parties you become jealous because you feel they're flirting. It's easier for you to blame your partner for flirting instead of looking at your own behavior, which you're afraid is similar to flirting. You might also accuse your partner of flirting and become jealous when they're talking to a certain person—the same person that you have a little crush on.

Another cause is known as internalized behavior, which is when you learned about jealousy at an early age. For example, you saw your mother get jealous every time your father talked about another woman in a pleasant manner, such as calling her beautiful. Your mother became jealous because your father never complimented her in that way. Therefore, you start to act the same way when your significant other calls someone beautiful or handsome.

Another cause is your history. You might have broken up with your ex because they cheated on you and now you worry your partner will do the same thing. This reasoning also ties into lack of self-confidence because learning that your significant other cheated on you causes you to blame yourself. Therefore, your self-confidence suffers and this trails into your next relationship. It's not always easy to realize that your new partner isn't like your old partner. This can take time but if you don't come to the realization early enough, you can damage your relationship. Do your best to remember that everyone is different and keep the lines of communication open.

Another reason is that you're trying to protect yourself. In other words, the more you're aware of your partner's behavior, the more you can protect yourself from anything bad happening. This means that you won't have to deal with a cheating partner again or you won't have to worry about suddenly being left alone. Unfortunately, your method of thinking won't keep you from getting hurt again. In fact, you're not really protecting yourself at all. You're more likely to create a toxic relationship.

Sometimes your jealousy is warranted. Your partner is showing signs that they have or are cheating on you. When this happens, it's natural to feel jealous, hurt, and react in irrational ways from time to time. However, the best step you can do is to remain calm and be honest with your partner. Even if you feel that they're not being honest with you, there's nothing that you can drastically do to change their behavior. Always remember that the only person you can control is yourself. You can control how you act and what you say. You can control what you decide to do in this situation, you can't control what your partner is doing, thinking, or feeling.

What to do about your jealousy

While you've learned the bad news about jealousy, there is good news —you can take action and overcome your jealousy. Of course, you'll still have pangs of jealousy during the course of your relationship, but that's better than having jealousy ruin your relationship or anyone's life. There are a lot of steps you can take to manage your jealousy and you want to focus on what's best for you, your partner, and your relationship.

One of the first and most important steps for you to take is to be open and honest in your relationship. Yes, there will be times when this becomes painful, especially when you start working through your past trauma. But, the more effort you put forth to create a healthy and happy relationship the stronger it'll become.

It's important to talk to your partner about your issue with jealousy. Even if you don't understand all of the reasons yet, you should still talk about the information that you know and understand. Discuss a plan with them so you can learn to manage your jealousy. For example, talk about going to therapy or other steps you can take. Talk to them what they can do to help you note when you're taking it too far so you and your partner don't start arguing.

Another factor to remember when it comes to opening up the lines of communication is that you'll find yourself revisiting discussions. While this might become frustrating at times, especially if you don't feel that your partner truly hears what you're saying, revisiting conversations is also helpful. First, it keeps you and your partner on task with any plan you make on learning how to manage your anxiety and jealousy. Second, it reminds both of you about the boundaries you set. Third, it helps you and your partner feel more comfortable and gives both of you peace of mind because you're working through a difficult situation. You'll be amazed at how strong your relationship becomes when you start communicating often and honestly.

Once you start working on your communication, you can start building trust. One of the biggest reasons people become jealous is because there's lack of trust. Fortunately, there are a lot of trust-building exercises you can work on with your partner. Another benefit of these exercises is you'll open the lines of communication. You'll also find yourself more comfortable with your partner, which will also help strengthen your relationship.

It's also a good idea to give your partner a little extra tender, loving care after you've opened the lines of communication. Your partner is struggling with your jealousy just like you are and they need to know that they're helping you. You're not the only one who will question if you're doing something wrong in your relationship. Let your partner know how they're helping you by communicating this information with them. Don't just focus on the struggles of jealousy, you also want to celebrate any milestones and accomplishments on your journey to managing your jealousy.

The first exercise to focus on is to get to know yourself. It's easier to be honest with your partner when you're honest with yourself. This can become difficult because you'll notice some of your faults that can easily break down your self-esteem. The best step to take during this moment is to remember that everyone has their faults, they don't define who you are, and you can work on them. For example, if you realize that you tend to get angry quickly and this pushes your partner away to the point that they're afraid to be honest with you at times, you can start looking at why you have a quick temper. Did you grow up with a parent who became angry quickly? Are you stressed? Do you feel that becoming angry is the only way your partner listens to you? The deeper you go, the easier it is to try to find ways to help you reach your best self.

A second exercise you can do to build trust is to let each other go through your phones, laptops, iPad, or any other device. This is an exercise that I've given to many clients and it's proven to help them build trust. The foundation to this trust exercise is that when you have nothing to hide, you don't care about your partner going through your phone. The trick is you need to continue to manage your jealousy so you don't become overwhelmed when you see your partner texting someone else.

A third exercise that I often include in my therapy sessions is to tell my clients to take turns planning a date night. When you're the jealous one, you want to have all of the control. So, giving your partner control by starting with a small task like planning a date night helps you feel relieved and build trust. Plus, it's another way that will make you feel special to your partner so you can start to focus on the feeling of love and care instead of jealousy.

Another step to take is to focus on becoming your best self. What I mean by reaching your best self is to set up goals that tell you who you want to be. Take a moment to think about the best person you can be and write down a description of this person, but be realistic. Remember, you're not aiming for the perfect person because this will put too much pressure on you, causing this step to backfire. Instead, you want to focus on the pieces of you (good and bad) that you want to work on. For example, you want to increase your self-esteem so you'll focus on techniques to help with that. You might want to focus on talking to your partner more as you realize you quickly shut down during conflict, so you start to focus on ways to communicate and decrease your anxiety during conflict. By focusing on you, you'll start to focus on your relationship.

Sit down with your partner and talk about boundaries. This is often something that couples don't do because they don't think about it. First, it's not something that you're taught to do. Second, like most people, you automatically assume that your partner understands the boundaries. But this isn't true. Neither you nor your partner can read minds, so you need to sit down and talk about boundaries in a clear and calm manner. Discuss what you feel is acceptable and what isn't. What do you feel your role is in the relationship and what's the role of your partner? Make a list of questions to help you and your partner talk about boundaries and then compromise. It's not always easy to compromise when your values are in the mix, which they often are with boundaries, but you need to keep an open mind. This doesn't mean that you drop your values or beliefs. It means that you realize your partner had a different upbringing than you. Their values and beliefs are just as important as your values and beliefs.

It's something that most people do—compare their current relationship with their past relationship. As I stated above, this is one of the main causes of jealousy and the only way to overcome it is by learning to stop comparing your relationships. Other than reminding yourself that your current partner is different from your ex, you can also remember that each relationship is unique. One way to stop comparing is to reflect on your past relationship. Ask yourself what you didn't like and what you don't want repeated in your current relationship. Then, you need to communicate this information with your partner. Be open and tell them how you were hurt and what happened. Yes, you'll feel like you're opening up old wounds, but you're also working on healing them.

Finally, never be ashamed or afraid to seek therapy. Pathological jealousy is dangerous for yourself and your partner. It can border on relationship abuse without you even realizing what's happening. Taking the step to reach out for help proves that you're a strong person who wants to do everything you can to better your life, the life of your partner, and your relationship. Be proud when you take this step and don't let anyone hold you back.

Chapter 4:

Fear of Abandonment - Your

Partner's Not to Blame

You learned a bit about fear of abandonment in Chapter 3. You learned that while many people confuse jealousy and fear of abandonment, they are very different. You also learned one of the most important realities of this fear —it goes much deeper and is more all-encompassing than any jealous episode.

Where Fear of Abandonment Comes From

Your fear of abandonment can come from many causes. You might not even have an idea where it comes from at this moment. You might have a stronger idea after you read this chapter, but this doesn't mean that you'll have an exact idea and that's perfectly fine. You might need to take time to reflect on your childhood and past relationships to begin to understand. You might also need to contact a therapist for additional help. Don't worry about how long it takes you to reflect and learn or the need to contact a therapist. Always be proud of the steps you're taking to build a healthier life for yourself and your partner.

One reason is you have experienced the death or the loss of someone near and dear to you. This person was a huge part of your life, and losing them felt like you lost a piece of you. In fact, it was too hard to process the loss, so you still haven't dealt with their death. Even if you lost the person 20 years ago, you're still struggling from the loss and this is causing you to fear the loss of another person that you love dearly.

This reason takes me back to one of my first clients. She was a young woman who came to me so she could save her relationship. In talking with her, I started realizing that she suffered from fear of abandonment. When I brought this up to her, she didn't agree with my assessment because she had two loving parents who did everything they could for her. It didn't start to click for her until she told me that she only lost one person in her life and that was her grandfather, who she was extremely close to. He passed away suddenly when she was 12 years old. I'll never forget how she looked me right in the eyes and said, "I couldn't look at him in the casket. I couldn't see him that way. I wanted to remember how he was when he was alive. I haven't even been to his grave in all these years." This client never truly dealt with her grandfather's death and it still affected her deeply, even 15 years later. She felt that her grandfather would have loved her partner. She also talked about how much her partner reminded her of her grandfather, which is one reason she feared losing him so greatly.

Another cause is past neglect or parental abandonment. Even if your parents were both physically in your life, it doesn't mean that they emotionally and psychologically gave you what you needed as a child. This can make you feel that your parents abandoned you, even if you won't admit it because it sounds silly or is difficult to accept. For example, if you felt that you couldn't talk to one or both of your parents about problems in your life or that you couldn't express your emotions, you can suffer from fear of abandonment.

Another cause of this type of fear is abuse. It doesn't matter if it's physical, emotional, mental, sexual, or verbal because all types of abuse can lead you to fear of abandonment. Look at it this way, if you don't emotionally and psychologically get what you need from your parents as a child, you worry that other people will treat you the same way. You fear that you'll be left alone and you believe that being with someone, no matter how they treat you, is better than being alone. This same method follows a person who was abused by a caregiver during their childhood or even in a past romantic relationship.

Poverty is another cause because it's known as a serious contributor to long-lasting trauma. At this point, it's important to note a distinction between growing up poor and living in poverty. When you're poor, your parents might receive aid from the state to help them buy groceries or get free meals for you at school. However, most of the bills get paid every month and you tend to continuously live with running water and electricity. You usually don't worry about if you'll eat that day because your parents always do what they can to ensure there's a meal on the table. When you grow up in poverty, you don't always know if you'll eat. You don't always have electricity and some people don't always have running water. You also have to worry about the environment outside of your home because it's not safe. While this can be an issue when you grow up poor, it's more common when you're living in poverty. Because you don't get what you need as a child, you start to worry about people leaving you, especially when they care for you. You also worry about losing the good parts of your life, including living in a good neighborhood or having food in your home at all times.

The loss of a significant and important relationship in the past is another cause. This can be any relationship from a parent walking out on their family to an ex partner that you broke up with recently. This relationship is usually with someone that you felt would be in your life as long as possible, but it didn't work out this way. This is usually thought to be the most common cause of fear of abandonment but it's not any more important than the other causes discussed. In fact, dealing with abuse or neglect are more common than the loss of a significant relationship.

Signs of Fear of Abandonment

Fear of abandonment is not talked about like jealousy. Because it's a popular topic, you understand jealousy and have a general idea what it feels like, but it's not the same for fear of abandonment. You might have an idea about what it is but you really don't understand the signs of it.

In general, you might read that fear of abandonment comes from issues you have with abandonment. It's a type of anxiety that you feel when you worry that someone you love and care about will leave you. You also read that it means you're more likely to cheat or accuse your partner of cheating. It increases your anxiety and you can quickly become a person that you don't recognize if you don't learn how to control your fear. While all of this information is true, there's a lot more to your fear and there's a lot of other signs that point to it.

First, you might have had fear of abandonment as a child. It's normal for babies and toddlers to have this fear, but you won't remember it at this age. If you ever remember worrying that your parents, grandparents, or someone else would leave you at a young age, you've had this type of fear for years. Either you didn't grow out of the fear as a toddler for some reason or you developed the fear later but don't understand why.

General Anxiety Disorder (GAD) is another sign that you have fear of abandonment. This is a type of mental illness that millions of people struggle with every day. When you have GAD, you don't really need a reason to worry about your partner leaving you. The little anxiety monster that you have in the back of your head will put the thought into your brain. From there, your GAD will take care of the worry and you'll develop fear of abandonment. While it takes awhile for the fear to develop this way, GAD can be a sign and a reason for your fear. However, it's important to note that just because you have GAD doesn't mean that you have this type of fear. You want to pay attention to the many other signs before you diagnose yourself with fear of abandonment.

Another sign is that you become attached to someone quickly, yet you can walk away from the relationship just as quickly. You do this because the worry you feel about them leaving you makes you believe that leaving first is the best option. In a sense, you're protecting yourself from getting hurt by leaving them and acting like you never really cared about them. It's important to note that when you follow this direction, you're going to feel sad or depressed for a period of time, especially if you were falling in love or already in love with the person. However, your fear of abandonment is so strong that it outweighs any other feeling, which means your fear stays in control.

A lack of long-term relationships is another sign. This ties into the third sign as you normally leave a relationship before it has a chance to become long-term. Take time to reflect on the history of your relationships and try to remember how long they lasted. If you noticed that you haven't been in a relationship for over a year, you might have fear of abandonment.

Another sign is that you aim to please your partner. You want to do everything you can to make sure that they won't leave. For example, you might feel like you need to walk on eggshells so you don't make them annoyed or irritated by your behavior. You might "give in" to them no matter what their request is. For instance, you know that all the money you've made from your job needs to go to bills but your partner wants to buy a new power tool. Even though the tool isn't a necessity, you agree to let him purchase it and try to find a different way to ensure the bills are paid.

Clinginess is another sign. You probably don't realize how clingy you are, but your partner might complain about it from time to time. For example, they might hint that they need a little bit of space. But, 'clingy' doesn't just mean that you need to be close to them physically. It also means that you need to connect with them over the phone or through social media throughout the day. You might find yourself texting or calling them several times a day and becoming frustrated or worried when they don't answer right away.

You believe that you're the cause of every breakup. Even if your ex told you that you're not at fault or you had friends tell you that it's not your fault—you feel that it is. It's common for people who struggle with fear of abandonment to bring issues into the relationship that sometimes causes the other party to leave, but this doesn't mean that it's always your fault. At the end of a relationship, you'll find yourself saying that you're not good enough for anyone and it's better than you remain single so you don't ruin anyone else's life.

Feeling confused about your relationship is normal at times, especially when you suffer from anxiety. But when you mix fear of abandonment into this, your confusion gets worse with every relationship. You know that you have problems and not just because everyone does. You know you have issues that spill into your relationships because you don't feel right about how you act. For example, you find yourself manipulating your partner so they don't go out with their friends to the bar. You know that your partner hasn't given you any reason not to trust them and they're going with friends who are married. Yet, you still manipulate them because you know that being alone in your home while they're at the bar will be torture for your mind. This makes you feel emotionally and psychologically torn. You start to feel bad and you might ask yourself what's wrong with you. You question why you can't "get it right" or "treat your significant other better." You feel torn between what you think, feel, and what you know you should believe.

Another sign is that you have unrealistic expectations for your partner. For example, you demand that they respond to your text every time you message them or they pick up the phone every time you call. It doesn't matter what they're doing. Other unrealistic expectations are creating rules that they have to follow, such as not talking to their co-worker or going out with their friends. Even if you realize that you're giving them unrealistic expectations, you feel that you can't stop yourself because it's one of the ways you protect yourself.

You use emotional blackmail to get what you want from your partner. Emotional blackmail is a negative form of manipulation used to control your partner. For example, you might threaten your partner so they follow your rules. Other examples include making them feel guilty or obligated to do something for you.

There are four types of emotional blackmail that you can use. It's important to understand each of these types so you can take the right actions when it comes to managing your fear of abandonment. The first type is known as "the punisher," which plays on your partner's fear. You have no problem telling them what you'll do if they don't do as they're told. For example, you might give them the silent treatment or even turn to physical abuse. The second type is called "the self-punisher." This is similar to the first type but instead of punishing your partner, you punish yourself. You do this because you know what you'll do will make your partner feel guilty. The third type is called "the sufferer." You'll take your time when doing what you can to ensure that your partner does what you want because you'll hold something, like a threat or punishment, over their head until they comply. You'll make your partner emotionally suffer until they do what you want, such as withholding affection. The fourth type is called "the tantalizer." You use this method when you promise a reward to your partner for following through on your demands. The problem is, you don't always give them the reward.

It's important to note that the levels of emotional blackmail can vary and it's not a common sign for fear of abandonment. However, if you feel that you're leading your relationship down this path, it's time to seek therapy for your abandonment issues. A minor step toward emotional blackmail can quickly turn into a severe case without you realizing what's happening.

Jealousy is another sign of fear of abandonment. When you become jealous because you worry your partner will leave you for someone who's younger or you believe is better looking than you, it's tied to your abandonment issues.

Perceiving other people as a threat to the relationship is not only a sign but also ties in with jealousy. When you believe that someone else is a threat to your relationship, you become jealous when your partner spends time with them. It doesn't matter if they're just saying hi and making small talk, the person is a threat. Therefore, they can't have any part of your relationship. While some people are considered a threat to relationships, most people don't want to be known as someone who breaks up a relationship. They're generally respectful, especially if they're friends or co-workers. However, you can still perceive them as a threat.

Another sign is when you have obsessive thoughts about your significant other leaving. It's your biggest fear and something that you think about every day. It gets to the point where the thought can consume your life and there's not much else you think about.

You have a craving for constant validation. You need to know that your partner appreciates you and you expect them to tell you. For example, you'll often ask them questions about how much they love you and appreciate everything you do for them. If they give you any type of criticism, you immediately start to worry and fear that they'll leave you. Because of your reaction to criticism, your partner will start to tell you what you want to hear instead of the truth.

Another sign is low self-esteem and low self-confidence. It is important to distinguish between the two. Self-confidence focuses on your talents or skills. For example, if you have low self-confidence as an artist, you don't believe that you're a good artist. You don't think that people will like your work and you constantly criticize every aspect of your artwork. When you have low self-esteem, you don't feel good about yourself. You might suffer from depression and feel worthless. It is possible to have high self-esteem and low self-confidence. It's also possible to have low self-esteem and high self-confidence. But, when you struggle with fear of abandonment, you tend to have both low self-esteem and self-confidence.

Along with low self-esteem and low self-confidence, you feel unworthy of feeling love. While a part of you will know that you deserve love and to be treated well, the other part of you doesn't feel the same. Unfortunately, this is the part that usually wins out. It's this feeling that causes you to leave the relationship before anyone can tell you "I love you." If these words come out before you leave, you go into panic mode and find yourself leaving the relationship quickly. In fact, you might even tell your partner, "You don't love me. You can't love me."

You have a willingness to continue unhealthy or abusive relationships because you're afraid of being on your own. For instance, if your partner is physically, emotionally, or verbally abusive and you realize this but refuse to leave because you don't want to be alone, you could be suffering from fear of abandonment. You believe that living with the abuse is better than being alone for the rest of your life.

Another sign is you over-analyze everything. You might feel that you pay close attention to detail, but what's really happening is that you're analyzing everything that happens. From there, you continue to think about it because your mind races with all of the meanings attached to it. For example, your partner comes home from work to tell you that they'll be working the second shift for a while because they can make more money and that's where they're needed. You know that your significant other had the option to go to the second shift, so you start thinking about all the reasons why they made the decision that they're not telling you. You think about them cheating, wanting to be away from you for a longer period of time, and so many other negative reasons. Even though your partner gave you the reason, it doesn't seem right to you. You over-analyze this situation to the point that you're thinking about it for weeks—even after your partner goes back to their regular shift.

Repressed anger is another sign of fear of abandonment. While you might not feel that you have hidden anger deep inside of you, it's highly possible that you don't realize it. If you're like millions of other people who suffer from abandonment issues, you're quick to anger. There are also times where you'll deal with a similar situation and feel calm about it. Your anger won't rise at all and you can't figure it out why the situation makes you angry one day but not the next. Psychologically, one of the main reasons for this is because you have anger bubbling to the top before you realize. For instance, you might have had a bad day or a situation triggered your past trauma and now you're like a volcano ready to explode. Even if the situation that causes your anger is insignificant, it's a huge deal to you in the moment.

Another sign is that you choose partners that you're not compatible with or who you know can't be your partner at that time. For example, you might flirt with someone who is married or you'll find someone that you don't have anything in common with. Without realizing it, you purposely pick people that you know won't make good partners so you don't have to worry about becoming too close to them. You know that the relationship won't last long or become serious and this makes you feel better.

At this point, you might still question whether you have fear of abandonment or not. If you do, you can go back through the signs and score them by using the numbers one and two. You'll mark down one if you feel that the sign doesn't resonate with you and two if the sign does. At the end, you'll look at your marks. You don't need to add them up, but you should notice how many of each number you have. The more twos that you have marked down, the more likely it is that you're struggling with fear of abandonment.

Managing Fear of Abandonment

You know some of the main causes and the signs of fear of abandonment. Now it's time to look at how you can start managing your fear.

One of the most important pieces of information you can take away from this chapter is that your fear of abandonment is not your partner's fault. Even though you can find reasons why you worry about them leaving you, when it comes to the foundation that keeps your fear standing, it goes beyond your partner. Your fear stems from a deep-rooted issue that comes from your childhood or a previous relationship. In fact, it can stem from both. It's highly possible that you'll need to contact a therapist to help you through your deep-rooted reasoning as you might not completely understand without that help. Remember, you need to focus on yourself and build your inner trust before you can start building the trust in your relationship. Therefore, the best ways to manage your fear is to focus on yourself.

Even if you don't know the main causes of your fear or all of your signs, you can still start focusing on yourself. One of the first steps to take is to realize that you're worthy of love. Realizing this won't happen overnight. In fact, it can take years for you to truly come to terms with how much love you deserve from the people around you. But, you can start by simply telling yourself that you deserve love. You deserve the love that your partner is willing and wanting to give you. You deserve the love that you feel from your parents, friends, siblings, and other people who are close to you. Don't focus on the people that don't give you the love that you deserve, focus on the ones who do.

Another part of realizing you deserve love is focusing on how well you love yourself. Self-love is extremely important and often overlooked, but you need to take time to focus on loving yourself as this will teach you how to love other people. Furthermore, it'll teach you that you're worthy of love from other people. Once you start working on self-love, you'll find yourself feeling better emotionally and mentally. For example, you'll feel your self-esteem and self-confidence increase, you'll start to eat better, you'll ensure that you get the sleep you need, and start to take better care of yourself overall. Another benefit of all this is that you'll start to take better care of your family members. Dive into the power of self-love because this is one of the best steps you can take toward managing your fear of abandonment.

Another step is to become self-reliant. At the moment, you might feel that your identity is tied to a relationship. You need to cut this tie and realize that your identity comes from inside of you. It comes from your emotions, mental health, how you feel about yourself, how you take care of yourself, and what you believe. You can start by telling yourself that it's not anyone else's job to make you feel emotionally secure—it's your job. You should also tell yourself that no one can be better at being you than you. Do your best to focus on increasing your self-reliance but don't be ashamed if you need to contact your therapist and ask for help. Like with other causes and ties to your fear of abandonment, there can be a lot of deep-rooted meaning to your lack of self-reliance.

Start journaling about your fear. Starting a journal can help you learn more about where your fear comes from and what signs you have that you need to focus on. It can also help you come up with the best ways to manage your fear. The trick to journaling is that you want to focus on more than your day. While it's a great idea to look at how you felt about certain situations or how you handled events, you also want to reflect on your past relationship, childhood, and other pieces of your life. For instance, you can write down when you first started recognizing your fear of abandonment. Even if it was from reading this chapter, it's a start to improving your life and relationship. You can also discuss any times you felt abandoned by people in your life, if you blamed yourself for an ex leaving you, what behaviors you exhibit connected to your fear, and what you can do to stop acting on these behaviors.

Another step to take is to realize that you can't cure your fear. There's a part of it that'll probably always be with you. Therefore, the best step you can take is to accept them and learn how to control or manage it to the best of your abilities. It's also important to realize that life is full of fearful moments and some of these will show up in your relationship. This is nothing to worry about as it's like anxiety—it's normal to have little moments of fear. The struggle comes when you let your fear control you as this is when it starts to control your relationship and even your partner.

Creating a support group is another step. You might find this through your partner, family, and friends. You might also find a support group through your therapist. No matter where you find your support, you need to ensure that you're comfortable, honest, and open with them about how you feel and what you're going through.

If you've never lived alone, now is the perfect time to do so (if it's possible). Even if you take time to find yourself living in an apartment for a few months, it will help you learn how to depend on yourself instead of a partner. Of course, this isn't always possible, but this doesn't mean that you can't find another way to start depending on yourself more. For example, start doing tasks that you usually ask your partner to do for you.

Once you start to understand your fear of abandonment and work toward creating a more positive view of yourself and your relationship, it's time to start focusing more on trust. Not only do you need to look at trusting yourself, but you also need to look at trusting your partner.

Chapter 5:

Building Trust and Finding Your

Conflict Resolution Sweet Spot

Trust is one of the most important antidotes when it comes to relationship anxiety. Without it, your relationship will fail and your anxiety will become stronger. You'll find yourself suffering from signs of jealousy and fear of abandonment along with many other problems. If you're like most people, you feel that the reason you don't trust your partner is because of something they did. You'll look for any reason to try to understand your lack of trust. For example, if your partner came home late one night without calling, you'll add this to your list. Even if it really didn't phase you that much at the time, you'll cite it as a reason and make your partner believe that they are the cause.

Understanding Emotional Baggage

The truth of the matter is that most of your lack of trust comes from your emotional baggage, and the only way to work on building trust is to understand and own up to it. "Emotional baggage" refers to the insecurities and issues we've faced in our previous relationships. You've been adding to your emotional baggage for most of your life without realizing it. For example, problems in the relationship with your parents is a part of your baggage. From there, you added any issues from past relationships. All of this has accumulated in a big black bag within your heart and mind and it causes you to struggle in your current relationship. The good news is that healing is possible, no matter how much baggage you're holding on to. The key is that you need to learn to accept the baggage, realize you can't change it, learn to live in the current moment, forget people who hurt you (including yourself), and let go of the things that you can't change.

The first step to working through your emotional baggage is to understand where it comes from. You need to know what type of emotional baggage you have accumulated through the years. There are many different types and each one comes from a certain point within your life. This means that you can have more than one type. For example, if you grew up in a dysfunctional family, you have this type. If you've suffered through domestic violence in a relationship, you also have this type.

Mental health is one type of emotional baggage. This usually happens after you've seen your doctor or therapist and they diagnose you with a mental illness, such as depression, General Anxiety Disorder, or Bipolar Disorder. It doesn't matter how insignificant in your life that disorder might be to you, it can still create baggage for several reasons, from the way society views mental health to the way you were raised to think about mental illnesses.

Mental illness can easily consume your life. For example, you struggle with anxiety every day. It doesn't matter if you're about to make a phone call to pay a bill or if you're about to open an email about a potential job offer, you feel anxious. You might even feel anxious when you need to talk to your parents because of past trauma from your childhood. When it comes to managing your mental health every day, it's exhausting. You feel drained quickly and this adds to your baggage. You also start to feel like a burden to people, worthless, and even become embarrassed about your mental health.

The reality is, when you're dealing with mental disorders, you need more reassurance than other people. Don't be ashamed to talk to your close friends and family members about what you go through on a daily basis. They can help you when it comes to your struggles and this will start to help you believe that you can trust them. It's also a good idea to contact a therapist as they can help you understand your psychological disorder and help you learn techniques to better manage it.

Fear is another type of emotional baggage that can come from one or several traumatic events. For example, if you found yourself trapped in a hostage situation, you carry this baggage with you. Even if you had an uplifting childhood and positive relationships, you can still suffer from this one event. Fear is one of the strongest human emotions and it triggers our "fight or flight" response, which jumps into our mind every time we turn back the clock and think about the traumatic memory.

The biggest problem with fear is that when you don't work through it, it becomes your biggest challenge. It starts to limit what you believe you can do in your daily life. You'll start to believe that you can't attend college because you won't succeed. You can struggle to hold down a job or keep focused on projects. You can even become afraid of having a relationship so you keep to yourself and become anti-social.

Along with fear, you can also have *guilt* as your emotional baggage. Like fear, this can develop from one traumatic event or several. It also follows you through life and keeps you from accomplishing your potential. Guilt will make you imagine situations that aren't true. For example, you feel that you're always a disappointment to your partner.

Dysfunctional family baggage is another type. This is the most common form of emotional baggage because the family unit we grew up with becomes our core. When you grow up walking on eggshells because of abuse, constant yelling, or negative emotional patterns, you carry these parts of your childhood with you throughout your life. You might feel that "it's over" once you move out of your parent's house, but you still have the baggage that you've been carrying for years. The biggest problem with this baggage is that with a dysfunctional childhood environment, you learn some of the wrong lessons in life. For example, if your parents solved arguments by yelling at each other and one storming out of the house you start to believe this is how you deal with conflict. You need to work through this baggage so you can learn how to resolve your conflicts in a manner that's better for your relationship.

Traumatic or abusive relationship baggage can come from any relationship that you have. For instance, if your parents abused you then you carry this baggage from your childhood. However, you might not accumulate this baggage until a past relationship where your partner abused you. There is also the option that you carry the emotional scarring from both of these situations. Even if a relationship didn't last long, you can still carry this baggage with you. You also need to note that just because you left the relationship doesn't mean that you let go of the baggage. The effects of living through an abusive relationship make you feel raw and emotionally drained. Your self-esteem is low and you don't feel worthy of love.

Regret is the final form of emotional baggage. You constantly have "what if" thoughts and you start to look at how you could have changed certain situations. For example, you regret ruining a previous relationship by cheating on your partner so you stay in your current unhealthy relationship because you don't want to make the same mistake of leaving. Regret can make you stop living your life in the present and even keep you from making decisions for your future.

Once you decide to grab a hold of your emotional baggage, it's time to focus on managing it so you can start to build trust in your relationship. While you might feel it's easier to place your baggage on a top shelf and pretend you don't see it, emotional baggage can limit you in several ways. Not only will it stop you from building trust in your relationship, but you'll also find yourself carrying around negative energy. Think of your baggage as an energy zapper. As you walk around and go through your day, you start to feel more tired as your energy wears down. This is because your baggage zaps all of your energy away.

Noticing you're unable to fully commit to a relationship is another damaging effect of emotional baggage. You also struggle to commit to a job, education, and other situations in your life. In fact, you rarely finish a project that you start.

You find yourself comparing your current partner to your previous partners or even your parents. For instance, if you were abused in a past relationship whenever you did something to upset your partner, you'll expect this in your current relationship. Therefore, you notice when your partner's becoming upset and will take the necessary steps to protect yourself from harm, even if your partner has never shown any signs of abuse.

Like with fear of abandonment, you suffer from lack of self-esteem. Even if you have a job you're great at, you're getting excellent grades in school, and your partner is always complimenting you, your self-esteem is low. When you carry emotional baggage with you, you remind yourself of the pain other people put you through. For example, if your father constantly criticized you, called you stupid, and verbally abused you, these words follow you. Instead of hearing your partner tell you that you're smart and talented, you hear your father's words. Even if you try to believe the words your partner says, your father's words are louder and bigger. They control your self-worth.

To build trust, you need to start letting go of your emotional baggage. You need to work through all of the effects that follow you. Fortunately, there are several techniques you can use to start building your self-worth, trust in yourself, and then trust in your relationship.

First, you need to learn to live in the present. This means that you don't project past failures onto your current partner or relationship. You don't focus on the words that your parents or past partner told you. Instead, you focus on the words that your current partner says. Like most techniques, this is one that you'll need to follow for years and it'll take time to start noticing the results. It means that when your emotional baggage jumps up at you, you accept it and tell yourself that it's in the past. You then turn and focus on something positive in the future, such as how you completed a project, your good grades in school, or the love from your partner.

A second technique is to start practicing self-acceptance on a daily basis. One of the best ways to accept the damage and start focusing on the present and your future is to accept who you are. It's true that your childhood family dynamics, no matter how dysfunctional they were, are a part of you. They helped form your personality. But, you need to remember that they don't define you. The only person who can let the emotional baggage cause problems in your current relationship is you. By accepting who you are, you can start changing yourself. You can look at who you want to become. Think of the goals you want to achieve and start working toward them. For example, your first goal is to focus on building your inner happiness so you look at the reasons why you're unhappy and solutions to help you gain happiness. You might decide that you need to seek professional help, start meditating, or change your mindset so you focus on positive thoughts.

A third technique is to write a letter. You don't need to send it, but you should either tear it up or burn it as this shows that you're releasing the emotional baggage. Writing a letter alleviates the conflict that confronting someone can bring up. It also helps you feel like you're taking a step toward healing and this gives you peace of mind. Along with writing a letter, you can also start a healing journal, similar to what you learned in overcoming fear of abandonment. Ask yourself a series of questions, such as what the person did, how the event started, and how long it went on. You can also write down how it affects you and even your plan to overcome the baggage.

If possible, get some closure to move on from your emotional baggage. It's not always possible, but it is always possible to learn how to manage it. You might need to seek counseling, but taking the steps to focus on working through your baggage and doing what you can to build a better life is a great step toward your future. Always be proud of yourself for everything you're doing to help improve your life and your relationship.

Building a Relationship Filled with Trust

Once you have a better understanding of your emotional baggage, it's time to start focusing on building trust in your relationship. There are many strategies that you can use to build trust so you'll need to focus on what works for you and your partner. You can start this process by reflecting on your actions, your partner's actions, and what you would both like to change. Sit down and talk to your partner about your self-discoveries and how you're trying to change them. Then, discuss what they feel about the trust in your relationship. Remember, you'll probably need to remind them to be honest so they don't sugarcoat anything. Even if they're comfortable talking to you about trust, they don't want to hurt you so they might not tell you everything. You both need to go into the conversation with an open mind and a realization that you might feel hurt during certain parts of the conversation. The key is to keep in mind that you're both working on improving your relationship.

One of the strategies you can use to build trust is to be direct when you're communicating. Tell your partner what you mean without beating around the bush. Don't play games or try to get your partner to guess why you're upset, sad, or feeling a certain way. They don't know how to read your mind just like you don't know how to read their mind.

If communication is a problem in your relationship, sit down with your partner and talk about ground rules of communication. For example, the first rule is that both parties always need to communicate respectfully. You might have a rule that neither person should communicate in anger. Instead, you're to request time to cool down and then revisit the conversation with a clear mind. It's okay to add rules as you start to build up your relationship or adjust them once you start communicating more.

You also want to communicate effectively. Be clear and honest about your emotions but also about what you're doing. For example, if you're going out to the bar with your friends for a couple of drinks, be honest with your partner. If you hear your partner tell you this is what they're doing and you start to feel anxious, let them know this is how you're feeling and work through it. Don't expect them to not go with their friends because you're anxious. Instead, take this opportunity and turn it into an exercise where you can build trust. It's fine to build the trust through baby steps. For instance, you might ask them to call you within a couple of hours to let you know how the night is going. Don't take this time to ask them a series of questions on who they're with and what they're doing. You want to have a general conversation. Then, talk to them again when they come home. Again, don't drill your partner about anything but simply ask them how their evening was and how their friends were.

Open yourself up to the prospects of a great love. Realize your worth and that your partner should love you just as much as you love them. This means you'll have to be vulnerable and let the other person into your heart and soul. It means that you'll need to let your guard down and let them see the true you. It's important to note that this isn't something that will happen overnight. It's a process that takes time. You might even find yourself closing up after a while because you feel anxious. You might fear that you're letting them see too much of you and this will cause you fear of abandonment. When you meet yourself at this crossroad, talk to your partner about how you're feeling and use strategies to help you overcome your fear.

Be consistent in what you're doing and what you say. Maintaining consistency is hard for anyone as sometimes you let things fall to the sidelines or you don't think that your partner will care much if you do something different this one time. While being inconsistent every now and then isn't too much of an issue, it becomes an issue when you're often inconsistent. It becomes a problem when you struggle trusting your partner. The fact is, being inconsistent leads to mistrust and can quickly break down a relationship. Therefore, it's essential that you do your best to stay consistent in the guidelines you set. If you tell your partner that you'll only be gone a couple of hours, make sure your home in a couple of hours.

Make important decisions together and define the parameters of each decision. This is a process of setting up healthy boundaries, which is something that will change and affect each stage of your relationship. This doesn't mean that you need to call your partner or they need to call you when they're buying a new outfit for an event. But, if you're looking at trading in your vehicle for a newer model, you want to go back to college, or you want to change your career path, you need to talk to your partner. Sit down with them and discuss the pros and cons of the decision and look at it rationally. Ask yourselves questions like "How will going back to college affect your relationship?" "How will it improve your life and the lives of your family members?" "What challenge will you face as a couple when you go back to college?"

Offer feedback and make it constructive if it's going to be negative. This means that you say it in a way that is respectful and you help your partner. You always need to be mindful of your partner's feelings. For example, keep the golden rule in mind which is treating other people the way you want to be treated. If you don't want someone calling you a name, don't call the other person a name. If you want your partner to talk about their feelings with you, open up to your partner.

Don't let emotional outbursts and anger become a normal situation in your relationship. If you're feeling angry, take a break and go back to the conversation later. If you're getting so frustrated that you feel like you're about to burst into tears, use a calming method or excuse yourself for a few minutes so you can regain your composure. At the same time, you don't want to say you'll do something when you're excited because this can lead to broken promises.

Give your partner the benefit of the doubt. Whether they have hurt you in the past or not before, it's time to push aside your issue and just believe them. This doesn't mean that you won't still question it in your mind or find moments where you're wondering if your partner is telling you the truth (but these thoughts should fade over time). But it does mean that you don't give your partner the third degree and you don't bring up the possibility that they did something when you're angry. You take their word and you do your best to sort through any issues and move on.

Learn to admit to your mistakes and say "I'm sorry." No one is perfect and you'll make mistakes just like your partner makes mistakes. Don't push aside your mistakes because you feel embarrassed about them or you think "it's not that big of a deal." If you expect your partner to apologize to you when they make a mistake, then you need to give them the same treatment. Even if you need to start writing it in a letter at first, this is what you do. Just find time to talk to them about it and build up your courage to say "I'm sorry" face to face.

But I've Been Hurt Before

It happens to everyone. You were in a relationship that you thought would last forever only to find that your partner cheated on you. You keep going back to those moments where your parents criticized you and made you feel like a burden. You've been hurt either physically, emotionally, or mentally before and now you don't know how you can move on from this pain. You know that you need to heal and move on for the sake of your present relationship, but how do you go about this?

First, you need to give yourself some time to grieve and recover before moving on to something new. Treat any relationship that ended in your life that you still cling to as a loss. Go through the grieving process just as you would the death of a loved one. This will help you move on from the relationship and focus on your current partner. It'll help you realize that your partner isn't like your ex and that it's time to look at your relationship with new eyes.

You also need to remember that trust takes time and that's okay. The key is that you continue to open up and take steps to improve your life and relationship. No matter how badly you want to start trusting your partner, you'll still be working on it in a few months. In fact, depending on your past you can still be working on building trust in a year. It's also a good idea to continue trust-building exercises throughout your relationship, not just when you need them the most. For instance, try a few exercises in a few years.

Do not project onto your new partner. You need to remember that the past is the past. Even if you continue to work through your past, keep an open mind when it comes to your partner. When you find yourself starting to make decisions based on your past relationship, take a step back and reevaluate the situation at hand. Block out your past relationship and think about your current one. Then, you'll make your decision.

Forgiveness is one of the most important steps when it comes to moving on from the past. You need to forgive the person that has hurt you and forgive yourself. This will take time, especially when it comes to the person who hurt you. It's easier to focus on forgiving ourselves than it is to forgive someone who caused you harm. Do what you need to do to forgive the person, even if that means confronting them.

Understand that you also have the power to hurt someone just like they can hurt you. It's a give-and-take scenario. The struggle is to realize that you're hurting someone because it's not always easy to realize. You really need to listen to your partner and sometimes read between the lines, especially if you've hurt them often in the past. For example, you grew up in a home where your mother talked down to your father. You started to see this as normal behavior in a relationship so when your partner did or said something that you thought was stupid, you would tell them. You called them names when you were angry and said many things that you wish you could take back now. Instead of dwelling on the past, talk to your partner and ask them for forgiveness. Don't make up an excuse to why you behave in this way, just let them know that you realize the hurt you caused them and you're doing everything you can to change it. You might even come up with a plan together where they help you notice when you're saying something that's hurting them. Again, this is a two-way street. If they're going to help you realize when they're hurt, you need to do the same for them.

Learn to love yourself first and foremost! In my book, this is the most important rule. I've said it before and I'll say it again because it's true— you need to learn to love yourself before you can truly love anyone else. This doesn't mean that you don't love your partner, children, friends, or family members now. It just means that you have love hidden in your heart because you haven't found true love for yourself yet. It's time to start tearing down your protection walls and learning how to love yourself so your true love can shine. It's at this moment when you'll truly start to nurture yourself, your partner, and your relationship.

Chapter 6:

Nurturing the Relationship and Strengthening the Feeling of Security

To keep your relationship healthy and happy, you and your partner will constantly work on nurturing your relationship. You'll focus on what helps strengthen your relationship and work out any issues along the way, including when your anxiety comes back to haunt you again. This is especially true when building trust and overcoming anxiety in your relationship. It's important that you realize now, this work isn't something that you'll only do in the beginning—it's an ongoing process that keeps the foundations of the commitment between two people strong.

The Secrets of a Happy, Long-Lasting, Anxiety-Controlled Relationship

There are many secrets to building a happy, long-lasting relationship that's anxiety-controlled. What this means is that you're never directly free of your anxiety. It will still jump out at you during certain situations. No relationship is ever completely free of anxiety, but you can learn to manage anxiety so you have a strong relationship for the rest of your life. It's important to note that the secrets I discuss here are ones that often come up with my clients in therapy. There are many others that you'll find more personal to you that I don't mention. The key is to follow the secrets that work for you and your partner.

Honesty is one of the most important factors in a relationship. Even when it hurts, you still want to be honest with your partner and yourself. If something is bothering you speak up and talk to your partner. Don't let it build up until you explode, tell them that everything is fine when they ask what's wrong, or avoid a topic because you don't want to hurt your partner. Even if you feel that your relationship is more peaceful when you don't bring up certain topics, you're going backwards instead of forward. Being honest means that you need to take time to reflect on your relationship now. Think about how you feel, what you like, and what you wouldn't mind changing. Talk to your partner about this and ask them to answer the same questions.

You always want to ask your partner questions. You don't want to assume and you aren't a mind reader, even if you've been with them for a long time. For example, you're talking to your partner about how they want to change their job. You know they have a good-paying job with great benefits, but they want to completely change direction. Their potential new career would mean less money and no benefits. As your partner is talking, you can't understand why they want to change. You want to know how long they've been thinking about this change. Don't keep the questions to yourself—ask them. The more you understand what your partner is feeling and where they're coming from, the easier it'll be to support your partner without strings attached, such as hidden negative emotions.

Another secret is emotional attunement. This is when you don't just listen to the words your partner says but you also feel them. You become attuned to their emotions and show empathy. For example, you're listening to your partner talk about their current job and you can see that they are stressed, so you start feeling this stress. You also feel that they are genuinely unhappy when they're talking about their job; it's like they don't have any energy for it anymore so they're just going through the motions. You then listen to them as they talk about a new potential job and feel their happiness and excitement as their eyes light up. You can notice your partner's emotions by noticing their body language, tone of voice, and what they're not saying. Emotional attunement will become easier as time goes on and your relationship starts to strengthen.

You need to make sure you set aside time to check in with each other. It's important to ensure that you're still on the same page when it comes to long-term goals, commitment, and values. You can talk about your relationship, what you feel is going well, and what you can improve on. By setting aside time once a week, it will become a habit and you'll start focusing on it throughout the week. However, it's also important to make sure that this isn't the only time you communicate or talk about any problems.

During your weekly talk, you can continue enforcing your relationship barriers that make both of you feel respected, taken care of, and honored. For example, you can check in to make sure that you're giving your partner the privacy they trust you will and that you feel comfortable and confident in your relationship. This is also a good time to discuss all of the boundaries that you and your partner agreed to. It's always good to have a refresher now and then as it'll help keep everyone on track and increase happiness, respect, and trust in your relationship.

You need to work on improving your relationship every day. As you know, relationships are a lot of work. You need to put forth the effort to make sure that you're communicating, listening, compromising, and completing your roles. Yes, there are days where you're just so mentally exhausted or an emergency comes up and your relationship takes a step back, but this doesn't mean that you continue the trend. If your relationship goes on the back burner today, you need to put it back on the front burner tomorrow. Also remember to communicate with your partner about how you're feeling and that you simply need a little down time.

It's important to have a spiritual component in your relationship. This doesn't necessarily refer to religion. It can mean that you talk about what love means to both of you and you find a connection in your answers. You look at how you can give back to the community or talk about your faith. For example, if you both believe in a higher power then you need to ensure this is part of your relationship.

Do your best not to fall into "the blame game" trap. It always takes two people to tango and this means that both of you are at fault. It's easy to point fingers and blame someone else when something isn't right or a mistake was made. It's at this point when you need to put your finger away and discuss what happened without focusing on who is to blame. You'll talk to your partner about what you can both do to make the situation better next time and then you can talk about something positive or what went right within the situation to help the conversation end on a good and strong note. Then, you need to let it go.

No matter how strong your relationship is, you can't avoid every argument. You can't ignore the feelings of anger over something that's happened or someone did. However, you can choose to take a break and calm down before you discuss the topic. You also want to focus on solving the problem together. In fact, research shows that 70% of couples say this is a major factor when conflict arises (Harrar & DeMaria, n.d.). The first step you can talk to follow this pattern is to not criticize each other. Realize that conflict is part of a healthy relationship and you can use it as a tool to make your relationship stronger by acting in a calm and rational manner. If you do feel that your anger is about to boil over, let your partner know that you need time to relax alone before discussing the topic. It might help to talk about a plan of action when you say you need time alone before a conflict arises so your partner understands that this is part of the process and it's best for them to take a step back and focus on relaxing their mind as well.

There is a difference between hearing and listening. When you hear someone, you know what they're saying but you don't really comprehend their words. You don't notice their emotions and you quickly forget what they said. When you listen to someone, you know exactly what they're saying and noticing how they're feeling. You are considering what they're saying and working it into your part of the conversation. It's important that every time you communicate, you're listening to what they're saying and not just hearing them. This also means that you'll want to turn off the television, put down your phone, and put away any other distractions that you can.

Another tip is to go back to when you realized you loved your partner. Discuss the reasons why you fell in love with them and why you still feel the same way. You can even talk about some of their annoying habits that you feel are a little cute at the same time (you know there is at least one). It's also important to touch your partner, such as when you pass each other in the kitchen or the hallway. All you need to do is gently graze their arm or hold their hand for a second. Physical touch makes you feel special and that you're loved.

When to Seek Therapy or Couples Counseling

If you cannot handle major issues on your own but both of you are still committed to making the relationship work, you should seek relationship counseling. As I've stated before, seeking counseling isn't something that should make you feel ashamed or that you've failed in your relationship. You should feel that you're doing everything you can to ensure that you and your partner stay together. You're fighting for your relationship and trying to make it stronger. This is an admirable step to take and you should both be proud.

But, this pride doesn't exclude the question, "Do we really need marriage counseling?" You'll find yourself asking this question multiple times and you'll probably give yourself multiple answers from "I'll wait until I can't take it anymore" to "I'll wait until I want to sign divorce papers." The reality with knowing when you need couples counseling is that the signs to look out for happen gradually. It's hard to notice that your relationship is in need of counseling because you become used to the signs and just feel that it's a part of your relationship.

One sign is that you stop talking to each other. You no longer communicate your needs on an ongoing basis. In fact, you might go a whole day or two without saying much to your significant other and not really think about it. You might even come up with excuses like you're both busy or you just don't feel like being around them. You always need to remember that communication is one of the cornerstones of your relationship and without continuous, strong communication your relationship will tumble down.

Another sign is that you can't put yourself in the other person's shoes. You no longer listen to them and you barely hear what they're saying. When your partner is talking, you're busy on your phone, laptop, or continue watching television. You only respond when they seem like they're becoming angry or tell you that you're not listening to them.

You play the victim often, even when you caused your partner emotional pain. It's at this point where you've stopped focusing on your partner's feelings. There are many reasons for this but the main one is that you don't feel like they're part of the relationship anymore. You might even question them if they still love you or want to be with you. When your partner does try to explain to you how they feel, you don't care to listen because you believe you're the victim.

Another sign is you start withholding affection and intimacy as a form of punishment. You might not even realize you're doing this, but if you tell yourself you don't want to touch your partner because you're angry with them—you're heading directly to this sign. It's normal to have moments where you need a break from your partner and you don't want them touching you, but they don't last long. It becomes a problem when you'll withhold your affection for hours or days.

If there is a lot of passive-aggressive behavior in your relationship, you need couples counseling. There are many signs of this from ignoring your partner to acting nice because you want them to feel bad for what they did. Another example of passive-aggressive behavior is purposely not doing something you said you would because you want to hurt your partner.

Your relationship needs couples counseling because you see your partner as the enemy. You're no longer on the same page. In fact, it might even feel like you're not in the same book. No matter what your partner does, you see it negatively and you start to believe that they want to sabotage the relationship.

Another sign is that you're experiencing serious sexual issues. You might even have another person on the side to help you release your sexual frustrations. It's possible to even see your partner as gross because of their hygiene choices or just because you don't see them as handsome or beautiful anymore. Even when you try to get yourself in the mood to try to light the spark in your relationship again, you can't make it happen.

Lastly, one of the biggest signs that your relationship is heading toward couples counseling is you see a spike in trust issues. You might have worked through some trust issues and felt that your relationship was holding strong on trust, but then you start questioning your partner again. You start worrying that they're cheating or not telling you the truth. You might even start believing that they don't truly love you anymore. Because trust is a cornerstone in the foundation of your relationship, you need to ensure it's strong to keep your relationship strong. Therefore, if you're lacking trust and you're not sure how to make it stronger within your relationship, you should seek couples counseling.

Chapter 7:

When Anxiety Rears Its Ugly Head

Again

I've mentioned this before but I want to mention it again because it's extremely important. Your anxiety is not something that you'll completely overcome. Anxiety is a part of everyone, no matter how calm they seem. It's a part of your relationship and it can be a healthy factor in your relationship. This means that even when you have established solid foundations, you will still face anxiety from time to time. The trick is that you treat it as an old enemy. You remember the tools you learned to build your relationship and you continue working on strengthening your relationship so you can manage your anxiety.

I've already discussed several tools that can help you manage your anxiety when it strikes. However, there are some additional skills and tips for people who are a part of a long-term relationship. These tips are helpful for when you find yourself struggling with another mental illness, such as depression. They're also helpful when you've hit a bump in your relationship and you're not sure where to turn.

First, you need to recognize the source of your anxiety. You can do this by asking yourself several questions, such as "Has something changed in my relationship to cause this anxiety?" or "Is something outside of my relationship causing my anxiety?" It's important to look at all factors to note where your triggers are because you can feel anxiety at work and drag it home with you. For example, you're stressed at work because you're juggling more projects than you're used to. You're trying to do everything to stay caught up, including working longer hours. Unfortunately, this is not only taking its toll on your mental and emotional health, but your personal life as well. You rarely see your children and your spouse, which is causing problems in your marriage. Even though you're not financially stressed, all the bills are paid, your children are cared for, and you can communicate with your spouse for a couple of hours every night, you still feel your anxiety creeping up. You can feel it when you're trying to tell your spouse about your day and listening to them. You feel it when your children ask you a dozen questions when you get home. Unfortunately, anxiety doesn't know how to stay in one place. It's not something that you can leave at the door of your job until you return the next morning.

If you write in a journal regularly, this is another way you can look at the source of your anxiety. It's easier than you think to struggle finding the source. By going back a few weeks in your journal, you can start to pick up where your anxiety started because it's easier to read the signs than observe them in your own behavior. You can also talk to your partner or friend and see if they noticed when you started to feel more anxious. The people who are closest to you can always tell when something isn't right. In fact, they might have already tried to ask you what was wrong or if something was bothering you.

Mindfulness practices are another great technique to take up. When you're mindful, you notice your emotions, thoughts, and actions. You're aware of your surroundings and you're in better control of your actions and words. While your brain isn't wired to remain mindful all the time, practicing the strategies can help you become more self-aware, which will also help you gain a better idea of what you want in your life. Of course, this will further align with your relationship as you work with your partner to develop goals.

There are several types of mindful techniques that you can utilize to increase this skill. The trick is you need to practice them every day. Luckily, there are enough strategies that you can mix them up and focus on them no matter where you are.

One strategy that I like to tell my clients to start with is to turn off all devices (television, music, phone, etc.) and focus on their meal. While I encourage them to talk with their family, I also ask that they eat slowly and enjoy their meal. They don't want to become lost in the conversation because they'll become mindless of the task. To practice mindfulness, you need to be aware of your task and focus on it. This means you notice when you're chewing, how big your portion is, how big the bites of food are, and how much you drink and when.

I have a lot of clients who travel and they always feel like this gets in their way of becoming mindful. In fact, I often hear, "I am so used to the drive that I don't even realize I'm close to work until I pull in the parking lot." It's easy to become mindless when you drive the same route five times a week. One technique I tell them to use is to notice each landmark on their drive. For example, if they drive through a town, a large building, a lake, a farmhouse, another town, and then railroad tracks, they need to make sure they notice each landmark. Another tip to use while driving is to decide to count all the red cars or the trucks you see on the road. Of course, if you drive a busy highway, it's best to focus more on something that doesn't take up too much of your attention. Always remember to keep your eyes on the road and the rules of the road in mind.

Another strategy that I think everyone should do is to wake up with a purpose. There are several studies that show when you start your day on a positive note, you're going to carry this tone with you throughout your day. One of the best ways to do this is to be grateful for what you have in life and think about where you're heading. To do this, you want to refrain from checking your phone, email, or turning on any device before you get out of bed. Instead, you want to start your day by sitting in a relaxed posture with your spine straight. It doesn't matter if it's on your bed or your favorite chair. Then, you want to close your eyes and focus on the sensations of your body as your muscles and brain start to wake up and prepare for the day.

Next, you want to take three deep and long breaths. Breathe in and out slowly as this helps your mind and body relax. The best way to breath is in through your nose and then out through your mouth.

Then, you want to ask yourself, "What are my intentions for today?" You can do this by thinking about your daily goals you want to accomplish. If you do this, remember to not make yourself feel stressed by thinking about all the work you need to complete to reach your goals. You look at each step toward your daily goal one at the time. Another way is to ask yourself other questions:

- What good do I want to do today?
- What can I do to have the best impact?
- Who can I help today?
- What can I do to take better care of myself?
- What quality of my mind do I want to strengthen?
- How can I be more compassionate to the people around me?

Next, you want to set your intention for your day. Even though you might want to pick more than one, focus on one as you'll work on your intention throughout your day. For instance, you might decide to take better care of yourself by only thinking positive thoughts. Even if you make a mistake or you don't perform your work correctly, you'll remove any negative thoughts from your mind and focus on the positive.

Finally, you want to check yourself throughout the day to ensure you're following your intentions. When you come to a check-point in your day, stop what you're doing, take a couple of deep and slow breaths, and look at your progress. Even if you notice a moment where you thought negatively about yourself, take time to forgive yourself and continue focusing on your intention. Always be gentle with yourself as mindfulness is a technique that takes time and patience. You'll also continue various exercises throughout your life so you're always building your mindfulness.

Another mindful strategy I'll share with you is to get active. That's right, exercise can help your brain stay off of autopilot for a little longer. Even if you set aside certain time to exercise now, you want to ensure that you follow the steps below to improve your mindfulness.

First, you need to be clear about your exercise goals and what you want to do. For instance, are you going to run, walk, or go to the gym. How long will your exercise session last? Where will you run or walk? You also want to keep in mind the sensations of your body. For example, as you lace up your shoes, notice how the laces feel along your fingers and how your shoes feel on your feet. When you stand up, run or walk in place for a minute so you can notice the sensation of this exercise. What you notice is the sensation you want to pay attention to when practicing mindfulness.

Second, take about five minutes to warm up. This is when you walk a little slower or you walk instead of run. You might also stretch a bit before you head to the gym. During this time, you not only want to focus on your moves and your body sensations, but also your breathing, which should be at a slow and steady pace.

Third, you want to settle into your rhythm. Start to pick up your pace and keep this speed for about 10 to 15 minutes. Don't stop to take a few deep breaths or a break unless you need to for health reasons or because you're building up your exercise routine. By noticing your sensations and speed, you'll find your groove and soon you'll feel like these few minutes just fly by.

Fourth, you want to challenge yourself. For example, you might pick up the pace or you might put more weights on the bars. Notice how your muscles and body feel during your challenge.

Fifth, you want to cool down. You'll take five minutes to start slowing down your pace or you'll decrease the amount of weights on the bars. You'll continue to slow your body down until your time is up.

Finally, you'll relax by finding a quiet spot and noticing how your body feels. You can focus on your breathing as it starts to slow down the more you rest. Don't stay in this moment for too long; about five minutes is all you need before you get up and continue on with your day.

Another strategy to use when you start to feel your anxiety come back is to ask follow-up questions. No matter how well you know your partner, there are times where they'll still say something that leaves you confused. Ask them questions so you have a complete understanding of what they said and what you need to do. Never be shy about asking any question, even if you feel it's silly. Asking questions means you're trying to do the best you can in your relationship.

Take a step back and stop over-analyzing everything. One of the biggest reasons anxiety jumps back into your life is because you start overthinking. It's normal for people to think that something is wrong when everything is going well, so your mind will automatically start over-analyzing. Just take a step back, take a few deep breaths, and relax a bit. Remind yourself that it's just your anxiety trying to come back into your life and that everything will be fine.

Do not ruminate on a thought for a long time as you're likely to blow it out of proportion. In fact, focusing on a thought for a long period of time ties into over-analyzing. Instead of wondering if you should or shouldn't do something, take action. Follow your intuition if something doesn't seem right because your gut is usually right. If you're worrying about something, talk to your partner.

Don't be afraid of having a tough conversation as these typically bring people closer together. It's common to sit back and think about what's bothering you for a few days before you decide if you're going to talk to your partner about it or not. The problem is, by the time you decide you've already started to drift apart from your significant other and they've noticed. They know when something is wrong, even when you tell them that everything is fine. Your partner wants to help you work through anything, even if it means that you'll open old wounds or you're anxious about an event in the future. Plus, once you open up to your partner and have the conversations that you really don't want to have, you'll feel closer.

Identify your triggers and share them with your partner. When your partner understands what makes you nervous, they'll pay more attention to the triggers. They'll be able to help you more easily because they know what's bothering you and what caused it. They might even catch it before you do and then you can stop the anxiety before it even comes to the surface. This conversation might fall under the "tough talk" category and you might need to space it out over time. For instance, if you have five main triggers, you can space it out with five different conversations. This will not only help you mentally, but emotionally because you're not facing everything at once. Sometimes it's best to work in baby steps.

You should also practice little acts of kindness towards each other. Just remember, this isn't meant to be a competition and you might need to have patience with your partner. You may even need patience with yourself because you're working through past trauma that's hard to let go and move on from. You can start by making it a goal to do at least one nice act of kindness for your partner every day, but don't let yourself become too controlled by a schedule. You want to also work on surprising your partner with these kindness acts. Soon, you'll start to feel these acts are more automatic and natural. It's also a good idea to remind yourself to be grateful for these acts every night. This means you might talk about what you enjoyed by a gesture or simply looking at your partner and saying "thank you" before bed.

It's important to remain in control of your feelings so you don't act out. For example, you're in a heated discussion with your partner and you become so angry you start yelling because this is your "go to" when it comes to this level of anger and frustration. This action will not help your relationship and it won't help decrease your anxiety. Instead, you need to focus on finding a healthy coping mechanism, such as taking a break for a few minutes or going for a walk.

This also might mean that you need to seek therapy for your anxiety disorder, especially if you can't seem to get it under control. The key is to find a therapist that is best for you. This might mean that the first counselor you meet won't be the one you continue going to for therapy. You might meet with five different therapists before you find one that you feel you can truly trust and are comfortable communicating with. It's extremely important to find the right therapist because they will help you the best.

One step to take to know if you've found the right psychologist is to ask yourself a series of questions. For example, "Do I feel comfortable talking to them?" "Are their credentials and experience right for my anxiety disorder?" and "Do I feel that they're professional and they'll help me with the right treatment?" It's important to note that treatment can mean talk therapy, which is a regular counseling session, or medication. There are some therapists that tend to turn to medication right away but you might disagree. In that case, it's important to look for one that focuses on talk therapy and will help you learn strategies to control your anxiety.

Try to get your partner involved in your therapy as well. This might not be easy, especially if they don't believe in therapy or don't think it will help them. It's important that you don't force your partner to join you, but you do ask them. If you feel that your partner needs a little time to warm up to the idea, give them this time. However, you shouldn't stop going to therapy, even if you do start to feel better. Many people with anxiety disorder continue therapy throughout their life because it helps them remain in control. If your partner is on the fence, talk to your therapist about ways that they could meet face to face without making it into a full therapy session. You can also try to gently persuade your partner by explaining to them that couples therapy is an incredible bonding experience that will increase the strength in your relationship. Your partner might need to see how therapy helps you before they decide to take the step. Be clear and honest when you talk to your significant other about therapy and ask them to be honest too. The more you understand why they don't want to go, the more you can help them through this time.

Conclusion

"People have a hard time letting go of their suffering. Out of a fear of the unknown, they prefer suffering that is familiar." - Thich Nhat Hanh (2014).

At the beginning of this book, I told you that I would not only explain anxiety, but get into detail about how anxiety affects relationships. Through the chapters, you've not only learned how common anxiety is but how it can negatively affect your life and your relationships. Together, we went through the external and internal causes of anxiety and what type of questions you need to ask yourself so you can start to focus on managing your anxiety.

You learned about anxious attachment styles and even took a quiz to help you understand if you're anxious or secure. You know techniques to help you rise above an anxious attachment style and reach secure attachment. While this won't happen quickly, every step you take will feel like an improvement in your life and your relationship.

Jealousy is one of the main ties to anxiety. It's normal to have a little jealousy in your relationship but it can quickly spiral out of control if you have anxiety. Jealousy is a powerful emotion that makes you feel you need to control your partner. You need to tell them who they can and can't talk to, if they can visit with their friends, and cause you to make rules that they have to follow. Jealousy can become so powerful that it takes over your mind and emotions. This leads you down a dangerous path in your relationship where you become manipulative or abusive. Fortunately, there are a lot of strategies you can focus on to help ease your jealousy. Through this book, you've learned what you need to do to take control of your jealousy before it takes control of you and your relationship.

Fear of abandonment is another powerful tie to anxiety. You not only learned where fear stems from but its signs. You also learned that you can manage your fear of abandonment. Even though you might feel that your partner is the cause of your fear, it's important to remember that there's a deeper meaning. In fact, you might have several deep-rooted meanings that cause your fear. It's important to address all of the issues, even if you have to seek therapy to do so, as it's the only way you can start to heal from your past trauma and focus on managing abandonment issues.

Once you have a good idea of where your anxiety stems from, you can continue working toward building up your relationship. This doesn't mean that you're no longer working through your issues, it simply means that you're starting to take control. You'll spend years talking to a therapist or focusing on management techniques. You'll be working on these techniques and focusing on strategies to build your trust and strengthen your relationship at the same time. The first step you need to take when you're building your relationship is trust. This is one of the main foundations of any relationship. It's also a major tie to your issues of anxiety as you struggle to trust people, even the ones who love and care for you the most.

You also learned several secrets to a happy and long-lasting relationship with little anxiety attached. These secrets are meant for you to bring into your relationship so you can start strengthening your connection, communication, and other foundational building blocks. But, even with these secrets you might still need to look at therapy. First, I understand it's hard for some people to admit that they need therapy. Unfortunately, many people feel that it makes them weak or a failure. But this is not how anyone should see therapy. Facing the fact that you need to see a counselor so you can improve your life, as well as the life of your partner, your family, and your relationship, is one of the greatest strengths that you possess. You should never be ashamed when you walk into a counselor's office.

Finally, you learned that no matter how hard you try, anxiety will rear its ugly head. It will come back and try to haunt you as the little voice in your head grows louder. It's up to you to take a break and understand why your anxiety is knocking on your door. You need to sit back and think about what's causing it to return and what you can do to manage it so it doesn't take control of you. For example, remaining mindful of your thoughts and actions is a great way to keep anxiety under control.

One of the most important insights from my book I want you to hold in your heart is that you're a strong person with high potential. You have your whole life in your hands and it's up to you to take the steps you need to so you can reach your goals. You need to take a stand against your anxiety so you learn how to manage it. Even when it seems impossible, trust me when I write that you have everything you need to manage your anxiety. Believe in yourself because you already took one great step in the right direction by completing this book. Be proud of where you are now and continue to look forward.

Thank you for choosing *Anxiety in a Relationship* to help you take full control of your anxiety and improve your relationship. I wish you the best and I hope that you found this book helpful. If so, please leave a review so I know that I helped you and other people learn how this book can help them as well.

CPSIA information can be obtained
at www.ICGtesting.com
Printed in the USA
LVHW031933070622
720714LV00011B/345